RACISM
and
AMERICAN
EDUCATION

Foreword by Averell Harriman

The Participants:

Harold Howe

Kenneth B. Clark

James E. Allen

Bruno V. Bitker

Kenneth E. Boulding

Lisle Carter

Christopher Edley

Erik H. Erikson

C. Clyde Ferguson, Jr.

Milton A. Galamison

Eli Ginzberg

Elinor L. Gordon

Leo P. McLaughlin, s.j.

Donald Ogilvie

Eugene C. Patterson

Thomas F. Pettigrew

Franklin D. Roosevelt, Jr.

Harry S. Rowen

Mitchell Sviridoff

Jerome B. Wiesner

C. Vann Woodward

HARPER COLOPHON BOOKS

Harper & Row, Publishers

New York, Evanston, and London

RACISM

and

AMERICAN

EDUCATION

A Dialogue and Agenda for Action

An Urban Affairs Book, under the general editorship of
Kenneth B. Clark

The Urban Affairs Series is sponsored by the
Metropolitan Applied Research Center, Inc.

RACISM AND AMERICAN EDUCATION. Copyright © 1970 by
Kenneth B. Clark and Elinor L. Gordon
All rights reserved. Printed in the United States of America.
No part of this book may be used or reproduced in any manner whatso-
ever without written permission except in the case of brief quotations
embodied in critical articles and reviews. For information address Harper
& Row, Publishers, Incorporated, 49 East 33d Street, New York, N.Y.
10016. Published simultaneously in Canada by Fitzhenry & Whiteside
Limited, Toronto.
First HARPER COLOPHON edition published 1970
LIBRARY OF CONGRESS CATALOG CARD NUMBER: 77-88629

Contents

Contents

Foreword

No issue in American life today is more important and more urgent than the subject of this volume—racism and American education. The Declaration of Independence proclaimed in 1776 that "all men are created equal," and the Universal Declaration of Human Rights, adopted by the United Nations General Assembly in 1948, stated: "All human beings are born free and equal in dignity and rights." Nevertheless, in our country today, this concept of equality is still too frequently denied in thought and in action. Racial prejudice remains in the minds and hearts of too many Americans; racial discrimination persists in our economic and social life; and racial emotions are unhappily fomented by extremists, both white and black.

The President's Commission for the Observance of Human Rights Year, 1968, was established by President Johnson in January, 1968, in response to a request by the General Assembly that all United Nations members commemorate International Year for Human Rights, the twentieth anniversary of the Universal Declaration. Its membership included both senior government officials and private citizens. The Commission considered the crucial role of education in promoting respect for human rights and established a Special Committee on Education to develop programs for expanding knowledge about human rights.

The members of the Commission recognized that the safeguarding of liberty does not depend alone upon federal and state action—legislation, court decisions, and enforcement—vital as these legal protections are. Over the long term, it is only through education that attitudes can be changed, prejudices modified, and understanding developed.

In order to explore the role of education in combating racial discrimination, the Commission convened a small conference of specialists on Martha's Vineyard, Massachusetts, in late July, 1968, and some of the participants reassembled in New York in December to review their conclusions. We are indebted to these distinguished scholars, educators, and other experts for devoting time and energy to these discussions. The Commission is also grateful to one of its members, Mrs. Elinor L. Gordon, for initiating the project and for providing hospitality to both of these meetings.

The twenty recommendations of the Martha's Vineyard conference, and the discussions underlying them, deserve the earnest attention of everyone—administrators, teachers, students, and the public—concerned with the imperative task of eliminating racial prejudice and discrimination. The Agenda for Action set forth in these twenty recommendations covers the whole of our educational system, at all levels and in all parts of the country.

In its Final Report to President Nixon, the Commission included, as the first of its Findings, the following statement: "There is need to increase instruction in the concepts of human rights at all levels in the educational system." This conclusion of the Commission has been affirmed in detail by the report of the Martha's Vineyard conference.

I commend this volume to all Americans who are concerned about the existence of racial prejudice and discrimination in our country and, in particular, to all those who are seeking means for eradicating these evils from our national life.

W. AVERELL HARRIMAN
Chairman, The President's Commission
for the Observance of Human Rights Year, 1968

Introductory Remarks

As a member of the President's Commission for the Observance of Human Rights Year, I was asked to undertake and develop a conference to be held on July 28, 1968, to mark the one hundreth anniversary of the adoption of the Fourteenth Amendment.

The Commission had been charged by President Johnson with the task of enlarging understanding of the principles of human rights. The original purpose of the conference, to discuss and endorse the UNESCO Statement on Race and Discrimination, which seventeen countries had already signed, seemed to me an inadequate task in view of the Kerner Commission Report, which had failed to gain serious official attention: in view of Martin Luther King's assassination several months before; and in view of the pending Poor People's March to Washington, D.C.

It seemed to me that we must make a meaningful effort to deal with racism in America, and I took as a point of departure some lines from the UNESCO Statement:

It is recognized that the basically important changes in the social structure that may lead to the elimination of racial prejudice may require decisions of a political nature. It is also recognized, however, that certain agencies of enlightenment, such as education and other means of social and economic advancement, mass media, and law can be immediately and effectively mobilized for the elimination of racial prejudice.

The school and other instruments for social and economic

progress can be one of the most effective agents for the achievement of broadened understanding and the fulfillment of the potentialities of man.

It seemed obvious that we must plan future action for significant change in American education. Anything less would be an act of cynicism. I suggested this to Kenneth Clark and outlined my plans for the conference: that we use no background papers, but only the Kerner Report section on education; that we assume a consensus of purpose, beginning where most conferences end, and discuss only plans for action. Dr. Clark, tired as he was, reacted with excitement and prepared a working agenda.

We selected Martha's Vineyard, hoping that the relaxed surroundings and air of detachment from daily pressures would encourage thought and probing discussion.

The agenda was prepared by Kenneth Clark and Harold Howe, as a skeletal frame—as a point of departure. Our hope was to produce one or more workable plans which would stimulate positive change in America relatively quickly. As it turned out, we were pleased to find that some changes could actually be effected without extra funding.

We invited a score of individuals of outstanding reputation in a wide diversity of professions—educators, scientists, economists, psychologists, and so on—convinced that every aspect of racism in American education should be examined, and that it could and must be altered if the goals of American education, on which American democracy depends, are to be achieved. This book distills and edits for clarity the dialogues of that conference, and presents our findings and agenda for action. Our work can only be regarded as successful if the agenda is implemented.

Without the generous efforts of Kenneth Clark and Harold Howe, the conference could never have taken place. We are enormously grateful to all the participants for their generosity, their caring, their time, their energy.

I should like to offer special thanks for the efforts and contributions of Rene Zucker and Stephen Schott, and most particularly of Joseph Lash.

ELINOR L. GORDON

The Participants

JAMES E. ALLEN. Assistant Secretary for Education in the Department of Health, Education and Welfare and U.S. Commissioner of Education. Formerly Commissioner of Education of the State of New York.

BRUNO V. BITKER. Chairman of the Wisconsin Advisory Committee, U.S. Commission for Civil Rights. Member, President's Commission for Observance of Human Rights Year, 1968. Member, U.S. National Commission for UNESCO.

KENNETH E. BOULDING. Professor of Economics and Director, Program in Social and Economic Dynamics, Institute of Behavioral Science, University of Colorado, Boulder, Colorado.

LISLE CARTER. Vice President for Social and Environmental Studies, Cornell University. Formerly Vice President of the National Urban Coalition and Assistant Secretary for Individual and Family Services of the Department of Health, Education and Welfare.

KENNETH B. CLARK. President of the Metropolitan Applied Research Center, Inc. Member of the New York State Board of Regents, and Professor of Psychology at City College of New York.

CHRISTOPHER EDLEY. Program Officer in charge of the Government and Law Program at the Ford Foundation.

ERIK H. ERIKSON. Professor of Human Development at Harvard University.

C. CLYDE FERGUSON, JR. Ambassador at Large. Special Co-ordinator for the Civilian Victims of the Nigerian Civil War with the Department of State. On leave from Rutgers University, where he was Vanderbilt Professor of Law. Formerly Dean and Professor of Law, Howard University Law School.

MILTON A. GALAMISON. Professor of Education, Harvard University. Former member of the Board of Education of the City of New York. Minister of Siloam Presbyterian Church.

ELI GINZBERG. Hepburn Professor of Economics and Director of Conservation of Human Resources Project, Columbia University. Chairman of the National Manpower Advisory Committee.

ELINOR L. GORDON. President of the Citizens' Committee for Children of New York. Member, President's Commission for Observance of Human Rights Year, 1968.

HAROLD HOWE. Program Adviser in Education in the New Delhi Field Office of the Ford Foundation. U.S. Commissioner of Education from 1965 to 1968.

LEO P. McLAUGHLIN, S.J. Chancellor and former President of Fordham University.

DONALD OGILVIE. Director of School Volunteers and Executive Vice President, Operation Breakthrough, New Haven.

EUGENE C. PATTERSON. Managing Editor of the *Washington Post*. Formerly Editor of the *Atlanta Constitution*, and Vice Chairman of the United States Civil Rights Commission.

THOMAS F. PETTIGREW. Professor of Social Psychology at Harvard University. Former President of the Society for the Psychological Study of Social Issues, a Guggenheim

Fellow, and Chief Social Science Consultant for the United States Commission on Civil Rights report, *Racial Isolation in the Public Schools* (1967).

FRANKLIN D. ROOSEVELT, JR. Former Chairman of the Equal Employment Opportunity Commission and Congressman from the Twentieth Congressional District in New York during the eighty-first to the eighty-third Congresses.

HARRY S. ROWEN. President of the Rand Corporation, Santa Monica, California. Former Assistant Director of the Bureau of the Budget. Former Deputy Assistant Secretary of Defense for Plans and National Security Council Affairs.

MITCHELL SVIRIDOFF. Vice President of National Affairs at the Ford Foundation. First Commissioner of the Human Resources Administration.

JEROME B. WIESNER, Provost, Massachusetts Institute of Technology.

C. VANN WOODWARD. Sterling Professor of History at Yale University.

I

The Dialogue

The Dialogue

THE PROBLEM OF RACISM

Kenneth Clark: We agreed we weren't going to ask busy people to give up a busy weekend to come to yet another talkfest in which the obvious was being belabored and from which we would get the usual proceedings—tired statements of what's wrong, guilt, etc. I started to share some of Elinor Gordon's enthusiasm when she and Mrs. Zucker and others kept repeating that what we really wanted was to see if it was possible for a group of thoughtful people to come up with a statement of action in the area of education and American racism that would take for granted what we all knew—a point of departure rather than a restatement.

As far as I can see, our whole list of questions, which has been called an agenda, can be boiled down to three major areas of concern. The first, and one which we may not spend too much time on, if any, is What is the basic problem of American education and racism? The fact that race is a significant, if not *the* significant, factor in American education certainly no longer seems to be debatable. The determinants of this may not be too clear but are certainly part of the fact. The consequences are quite clear, certainly, since in the Brown decision the results of racist education in America, as far as the minority group youngsters are concerned, were clearly spelled out. No one seriously questions this now. There are, however, some insidious consequences.

I would like to remind you that in the preparation of the social science appendix submitted to the Supreme Court in the

Brown decision,* a considerable amount of attention was paid to the outcome of segregated education on dominant-group children. The court in its wisdom, however, chose to ignore this fact, but some of us still believe that it is an important part of the problem of racism in American education—namely, that not only are lower-status minority children damaged by segregation, but the pervasive component of racism damages in subtle ways the education of privileged children as well. The racial organization of schools in America from Head Start through professional schools perpetuates racism.

In the past one could look at this problem partly in terms of the desire and the will of white segregationists or supremacists, who took the initiative in supporting and insisting upon the maintenance of racial organization of educational systems in America. But we do have what seems to me to be an important new ingredient here: the rise of black racism has reinforced the traditional form of racist support for segregated organization of schools and the perpetuation of racism. The demand for separate schools is now coming from a very strident and articulate minority of Negroes, and this seems to me to be an extremely important symptom of the pervasiveness of racism in education and the outcome of a very complex manifestation of past racism.

This then leads me to the second main issue, which I think underlines the agenda before us: that when one looks at the problem of racism from a certain perspective one can perceive it as practically an impossible problem for educational institutions to deal with as such. The rationale for that perspective, and I have often heard it stated, is that educational institutions, like other institutions in our society, are merely reflective of the society as a whole. When educators give this rationale, they are passively accepting a limited role for education: education just has to do the best it can in dealing with

* *Brown* v. *The Board of Education,* Topeka, Kansas, 1954.

what is. This passive acceptance of the limits of what education can achieve has led to the proliferation of approaches to the problem. The various enrichment programs and special programs for Negro students, aided and abetted, of course, by the new black separatist courses, are simply a new form of the separate-but-equal—separate-but-superior—problem. I cannot avoid the temptation to express my own feelings: I believe that the very success of these programs tends to mask the basic issue and confuse it.

Another part of this issue is that educational institutions and educators have not really assumed an initiative in helping to free Americans of the tenacious, pervasive, and particularly the subtle components of the social disease of racism— and it is an education problem: education in the specific sense and education in the broader sense. It is a function of education to help to free human beings from the constrictions of superstitions, irrational fears, and hatreds, and it is a prime function of education, we believe, to attempt to liberate the human mind and the human spirit.

And the third basic issue, one which I suppose we would want to address ourselves to for the most part, if these first two are accepted: what are some realistic and imperative actions within the power and scope of educators and educational institutions? What are some short-range things that can be done? What are some long-range things that can be and must be done within educational institutions, with educational institutions taking the general initiative in terms of general public education? What must educational institutions do by way of changing perspective or taking risk and by way of resources—by way of reorganization of the institutions and systems themselves? What are realistic roles for public educational institutions and private educational institutions? What are realistic roles for federal and state governments. What can one expect from local organizations? And I think a very important question, if we are really going to be realistic, is What are the real risks and barriers here that make the difference between pious abstract goals and the possibility of implementation? What are some of the things that we can count on—resources, scholarships—which would make for a realistic program of action? And finally, what are our chances of success if we were to go that far, or would we even think about that if we are clear about these other things?

RACISM AND THE STRUCTURE OF AMERICAN SCHOOLS

Harold Howe: As a starter it might be worth while to try to keep focused on the institutional structure and its various alliances with the community and other elements. To the degree that we can avoid a rather extensive definition of the problem of racism, I think our time will be used better. At least among four or five of us with whom I've already talked there is a considerable amount of agreement that racism is widespread, pervasive, rampant, on the increase at different rates in different places, still very much evident in the education system, or what I would call the education "nonsystem" of the United States.

And it's around that concept of calling it a nonsystem that I'd like to make just one point. We can't address ourselves in simple fashion to a single decision-making level or policy-influencing level when we talk about education in the United States. We have people around the table here who represent institutions, people who are responsible for state departments of education, people with federal responsibilities. There are at least three levels of government with responsibility for education, and there is a thing called institutional autonomy that is highly pervasive among institutions of higher education, whatever that may mean. These institutions are jealous of their prerogatives and do their own decision-making on these matters. Therefore, I think we have to look for practical suggestions about what can be done at the various decision-making levels—at state levels, at federal levels, at institutional levels. And hopefully we'll direct our conversation within the institution, to what can be done by teachers, by students, by presidents, and by trustees, because there is, of course, within the institution itself a good deal of a hierarchy and various points of leverage in getting to the problem we're addressing ourselves to.

I'd make one additional point which I think is another way of getting at something you said, Ken, and it's this: it seems to me that education traditionally reflects the beliefs and values of the society. We're talking at this meeting about education's taking a posture which will change the beliefs and values of the society, if indeed these beliefs and values are racist in nature, as some of us perceive them to be. There are many of us and others who have been trying to put education in that posture, and it's been tough on education. It has caused education to be suspicious. I think we need to consider the practical implications for the health of the educational institution itself.

A more personal comment, simply because I have been involved at the federal level: the federal posture in relation to the issue of racism in education has no clear organizational expression in the federal government. It's a highly dispersed sort of enterprise. A series of agencies and programs is concerned about racism in education. No one has ever tried to bring them together or even to relate them to each other in a very rational way. There are the people who are concerned on the legal front, there are the people who are concerned from the Civil Rights Commission point of view, there are people in HEW, etc. And there are a variety of grant programs and funding programs that do have some relationship to this issue of racism in education now enacted and available as tools. But they, in turn, are not very well related to each other. Some advocate pulling all these things together and trying to strengthen them. But it is my experience in the federal government that if you create a single target about an unpopular matter, it soon becomes pretty well shot at. Therefore, it may be well to have many targets and keep them dispersed.

Ken, you, in effect, ask us to question, on a very practical level, what are the short-range and long-range specific attacks that will make a difference and can be made by federal, state, local, or institutional authorities.

James Allen: We take the position that it is the responsibility of the state to see that all have educational opportunities. There are many things you can do or try to do to assure equality of opportunity.

In the state of New York, as you know, the Commissioner of Education has a good deal of authority. He has a judicial role to play, in that anyone who feels himself aggrieved by the action of the local school authorities may appeal to the Commissioner. He has to hear the case just as if it went to court; his decision is final and not reviewable in any court or place whatsoever.

At any rate, New York has been committed as a state, a state education system—at least at the top level—to integration, to desegregating the schools, to removing every possible barrier to equal educational opportunity. We have now, for a number of years, directed every school system to present to us a plan for the elimination of segregation, and we have sought and received a modest amount of money from the Legislature to help the communities dealing with this problem.

But, as I said recently, the problem is so tremendous, and runs ahead at such a speed, that all these efforts New York has been making—and they have been considerable as states go, I think—seem not to make, at least to us, a great deal of difference. If your goal was to reduce the amount of racial imbalance in the school systems, our figures show that over the last ten years since we've really been making an effort we have been going backwards, if that alone is your measure. However, if your measure is a growing recognition of the problem on the part of the educational authorities, there has been, I think, some progress. At least in the very first meetings of school authorities in New York State on this subject, when we asked for a census report of race in the schools, it was a very coldly received request. Today I think the whole attitude, at least in terms of educational forces recognizing this as a problem, has been greatly improved.

But, what I'm finding is that there are barriers built into the educational system itself—not just in attitude, but in the structure, the finance, the organization of the education system —that are very real when one tries to accomplish something.

One case came up just last week—some of you may have noticed it in the *New York Times* this morning—of a school district on Long Island, the first school district in the state of New York that has become something like 75 to 80 per cent racially isolated. An appeal was brought to me asking me to dissolve this school district, and I jumped in, thinking that here was a chance to begin—really to begin—to lay down a policy and then move. But we ran into so many conditions, fiscally, legally, here that we finally concluded we simply did not have the authority to dissolve this school district.

I have, therefore, gotten quite interested in the comment that Mr. [James] Conant threw out casually recently, and that is that the only way you're going to do something about these problems is to remove from the local level the power to tax, so that decisions, educational decisions, at the local level can be made in terms of educational merit, without having finance stand in the way, because that was really what happened in this case. It was difficult not only at the local level but also at the state level; because this particular school district has a bond issue of such and such. Districts usually have a different bond issue, the tax rate is different, there's no provision in the laws of the state as to what you do about the teachers when you dissolve a district, and many things of that sort. So I have thrown out the proposal: if we could move the financing of education entirely to the state and federal level, remove local taxation for education, we could then begin to draw up school district lines, and we could begin to set the structure up in such a way that the local people could exercise local initiative and local responsibility and local control in terms of educational merit rather than in terms of fiscal policy.

This, of course, is a long way off. It's a very complex and very difficult problem, but it seems to me from the experience I've had now over a ten-year period, that two things are most difficult: (1) What to do about changing attitudes on the part of the people—and this seems to me to be the basic education question. And (2) how to change the structure of the educational system so as to provide the conditions which will make possible a good education in an integrated setting.

Clyde Ferguson: I'd just like to follow up on one notion which goes back to your description of nonsystem. It seems to me one of the basic problems is the fact that the system itself, to use that current cliché, does respond to what we would call racist pressures; in fact, the localized system is so structured as to give it play in the formulation of educational policy. Some consideration might be given to radical systemic reform which would remove the multiplicity of levels which perform functions other than the achievement of quality education. It might also be necessary to distinguish the problems of racism, in terms of content and attitude, from the question of race itself. In terms of short-range operations, no doubt, race as a fact is so imbedded in the fabric of this country that it is impossible to pretend that race does not affect decisions. It is going to be rather impossible to talk intelligently about basic reforms concerning racism without talking about problems of the structure by which we actually operate the educational institutions.

I personally have a very different approach from some of my colleagues who are concerned about localizing and fracturing even further the educational structure. I believe it ought to be going in the opposite direction—ought to be going in the direction of centralizing.

I think we have the choice of two kinds of models: local government—the best government is the one that's most local —as distinct from a model like the structure that supports the common defense of the country, which is highly centralized and has a set of rather rigid central standards for minimum qualifications for the statement of goals, and the like. And education, to my mind, looks more like defense than like the problem of who's going to be the dogcatcher.

Kenneth Clark: You mean it looks more like defense in terms of what it *should* be like.

Clyde Ferguson: Of what it *should* be like. But I think a fundamental problem is the systemic structural problem, because we are dealing with racism as it infects the structure. Or in my mind, the structure that reflects the racist attitude of the society, which has built a structure that has let racist attitudes have a free way, a free play in decision-making. The only way to get at that is to deal with the problem of putting the structure back together, so at least we can find out who is making the decision, and the level at which the decision is made. To my mind that points to centralization.

I know that historically this bothers all these teachers, college people who don't feel that the flow of history can be reversed in terms of local responsibility, particularly for the lower levels of education. In fact, I think our history demonstrates this is not so. We had a national educational system. It's been private to a large extent, but, nonetheless, we've had a national educational system with national standards which have been restricted to a particular class in the society. I think an examination of that as a possible model for general education in the United States might be rather fruitful in dealing with the problems of systemic racism. This is distinct from the personal problems of attitudes—a critical problem itself, but one I think is separate from institutional systemic racism affecting decision-making now.

Eli Ginzberg: If you look at federal housing over twenty-five years—urban renewal and so on—do you conclude from that, that a better shake for minority groups is an inevitable concomitant of centralization?

Clyde Ferguson: No. I once wrote an article on why that fails. I won't bore you with it, but there are federal programs and federal programs. Housing has been pretty much like welfare —an ultimate federal repository for dollars—but the effective decision level has been local and for very definite political reasons. Housing more than any other field has been responsive to the kinds of local pressure which inevitably have meant racial restriction in the housing market; it is not truly a federal program.

Eli Ginzberg: Wherever the federal government has to deliver concrete services locally, it has great difficulty in performing that service effectively. It's best job is to mail checks, as in social security. That it can do very easily. When it has to deliver services locally, as in health or in education, or has to deal very concretely with local attitudes, as in the housing story, it has limited leverage.

Clyde Ferguson: I think that you're describing the result, when the decision as to how the program is to be administered has already been made and to what extent the local bias is to enter into that administration. I again go back to defense, where I think the government has functioned more effectively than in any other single area of federal responsibility, particularly in the social end of the defense establishment, as in housing, for example.

Jerome Wiesner: The most inefficient, wasteful system in this country is the Defense Department.

Clyde Ferguson: I will not speak to the question of inefficiency . . .

COMPETITIVE SYSTEMS AND THE POSSIBILITY OF STRUCTURAL CHANGE

Jerome Wiesner: I don't think the Defense Department is a model for anything. But I think the point Dean Ferguson is making is a good one. What we need to do for the kids we're talking about is to provide an alternative system, a competitive school system. One of the things that's wrong with education in the United States is that in spite of the fact that there is a private school system for a few kids, the majority of kids are a captive audience for the school system, good or bad. It's only a very few kids whose parents can afford it, who are fortunate enough to have some choices. Even there the choices aren't good in all respects.

We should give some thought to how we can create alternative educational opportunities for the kids in the cities, kids who are trapped in the circumstances we're worrying about, whether this be by providing alternative educational systems within the community, like one we are trying to create in Boston, or whether you do what some of the people at the Harvard Graduate School of Education were talking about at one stage—I think a very good idea—to provide either state or federal tuition subsidies for students who want to go to alternative private schools or other school systems. And possibly Mr. Howe or Mr. Ferguson agrees with me.

I think the problem is really to introduce some choice and some competition into the elementary and secondary school system. By doing that you'll break some of the crucial bonds and get to the problem. I think we also have to think about how to deal with the system that exists, because it will go on existing.

You've got two separate sets of problems. One is the sort of racism that comes from inadvertence. In a book about the Boston school system, *Death at an Early Age,* the author dealt mostly with people who thought they understood the needs of the black kids and were treating them properly while they were choking them to death. Maybe we should do what we've done in the science field. The National Science Foundation runs summer institutes for science teachers to try to teach them about the more modern materials. Perhaps we could have some summer institutes on racism.

Harold Howe: It seems to me that we could have such institutes. We have some now, but with very minor financing. We have, however, a relatively large financing that could be turned in that direction if we could get the people who control it to exercise the options. That's one of the problems in the decentralizing arrangement.

Harry Rowen: It seems to me that there are several really diverse objectives that we've been talking about. I would pick out three categories of objectives, though it could be structured somewhat differently. One category is those actions that influence attitudes directly or more or less directly—changes in history books, things that are done by the media, teacher training, sensitivity training, ways of getting at attitudes. A second category has to do with structural changes to promote integration primarily—equal access—there are a variety of mechanisms to do this. A third category is actions to improve the performance and quality of schools, overlapping the other two categories but distinct as well—and particularly for minority groups.

Some actions we might favor for one objective, we might disfavor for another objective. There are tradeoffs. We might have to pick and choose. We shouldn't assume that all of these are necessarily going to work in the same direction or be able to satisfy all objectives equally within a given set of policy measures. I would think myself, for example, that a system of various measures to increase the diversity among school systems could go a long way, depending upon what mechanisms are chosen, to improve quality, but they might also just make it tougher to get integration in private schools. There would be hard choices to make. But in any case these, it seems to me, are the objectives.

Harold Howe: I think if we could start in with Harry's first point—actions to influence attitudes directly—it would be very useful.

Thomas Pettigrew: Changing attitude is more of a subhead to your principal topic than a goal to be attacked point-blank. The only thing social psychologists have been able to find that really works—Kenneth [Clark] was beating at the truth twenty years ago, and people weren't listening—is structural change. The conventional wisdom is that if somehow you change people's attitudes, they will be willing to accept structural change. But in point of fact, it is just about the other way around. This leaves still open the question of how you achieve the structural change in opposition to these attitudes. To really do the job on a kind of fundamental attitude change requires structural change—and the sooner the better. Though I am a social psychologist and it is in my vested interest to think of things that aren't so structural, in respect to attitudes,

I've come around more and more to thinking that educational attitudes are just structure and then seeing what happens to attitudes. If you can desegregate schools you will achieve enormous changes in the attitudes of both black and white kids toward each other and toward themselves and toward the United States and the world. But how are you going to get structural change?

School construction of systems, as they presently exist anyway, is, I think, the critical item, and may be a first step or first couple of steps toward Jim Allen's hope of more and more fiscal responsibility to the state and federal government. But not as we now presently give money through the state and federal governments—not, that is, through single districts. Any businessman looking at public education would be horrified—some are now looking at it for the first time, and they *are* horrified—to discover that systems don't even buy common supplies together for obvious savings when they are all hard-pressed financially. The most elementary cooperation doesn't exist, but I think it could come about if federal and state aid systems, particularly in school construction, were based on incentives, so that no system got aid until it was cooperating across districts, particularly in metropolitan areas of the central city, and always as a partner.

James Allen: You really have to remove the financing entirely from the local level. You've got to take this away entirely before you can begin to decide where schools ought to be built, and to draw lines and things of this kind.

Jerome Wiesner: You might not have to take away entirely the amounts of aid some states are giving to their local school districts. The amount of federal aid, which is growing, may be sufficient to allow you to have the leverage you want without creating a tax-base problem—a devil of a problem, at least in some places. In Massachusetts we have moved to the point where the leverage that the state could have for the control of funds is very substantial.

James Allen: You can't change boundary lines and things of this sort very easily, though, unless you get rid of the fiscal aspect of it all.

Jerome Wiesner: You can give them big incentives for it; and, you're right, if you could get rid of the local tax base, it certainly would make a big difference. But I think that is probably the preface.

James Allen: We put up probably 70 to 80 per cent of the cost of school building right now from the state level. But that 15 to 20 per cent voted locally is what makes the decision.

Jerome Wiesner: You could change the rules so that you could have a bigger say in the decision.

James Allen: Oh, yes . . .

Harold Howe: There is no major federal program at the present time that reaches generally to the construction of schools. There *is* a major federal program reaching the construction of higher education facilities. And there's real interest in the Congress. There have been bills introduced. One, I remember, by Ted Kennedy, had a major construction component, designed somewhat in the fashion you're talking about, Tom. It would seem to me useful to consider that kind of thing as a possible recommendation from this group—essentially a premium on federal construction money containing components of joint school district planning around racial isolation problems. In a very realistic political sense if you had a construction bill which contained nothing but that, I don't think you would ever get it through the Congress of the United States. But you might be able to have an extra payoff for that and get it through and then have a lower level of support for normal school construction activities.

Kenneth Clark: I would like to go back to Harry Rowen's breakdown into the three objectives—the attitude changes, the structural changes, and the actions to improve the quality. Harry, where in this breakdown would you zero in on the problem of racism within the educational institutions themselves? Before I could buy this as the breakdown I would want to know where that would fit. Unless you could show me that the racism problem probably fits into the third, it might let the educational institutions—elementary, secondary, and higher education—somewhat off the hook, continuing to see themselves as passive reflectors.

Harry Rowen: I don't really think I quite understand the problem. I take these to be proximate and not so proximate objectives. It seems to me to be quite plausible to argue that the thing that really is going to make the biggest difference in racial attitudes in the United States is for minority kids to perform as well in school as white kids. Short of that one can't really make a big difference. If one came to hold that view—and I am not sure one would, but in any case suppose one did—by God, you would really work out a variety of things you felt could effect a big attitude change, either through curriculum or through integration itself. But depending on your theory as to how the present attitudes got formed and what it takes to change them, you would have a different type of program.

Mitchell Sviridoff: I want to present a contrary view. So far we've been talking about structural changes in the field of education. Just for the sake of discussion and maybe argument, let me present this proposition: everything that is happening today militates against the achievement of structural changes for integration purposes. The reorganization of state legislatures has not strengthened the voice of the cities; quite the contrary, it has strengthened suburbia, and suburbia is not very integrationist when it comes to housing and schooling. They are very integrationist when it comes to garbage collection or air pollution or things like that which benefit suburbia directly. So the attitudinal problem is complicated by the political problem.

And then experience—the disastrous experience—and Milton Galamison can testify to this as well as anybody, in trying to achieve integration has led to Negro leadership losing interest in integration.

Harold Howe: It depends on whom you're talking to.

Mitchell Sviridoff: I'm going to advance this proposition that the most—surely the most vulnerable—

Kenneth Clark: The most vocal.

Mitchell Sviridoff: Well, let me put it another way: If you tried to organize a Negro movement for integration in New York City today, in contrast to trying to organize a Negro movement for decentralization, for every ten people you get to the first meeting you would get a thousand to the second meeting. I'm not saying that this is the attitude of the Negro population—there is some evidence that it is not. A recent Bedford-Stuyvesant survey* suggests that this is not the popular attitude. What I'm talking about is the attitude of leadership, but the attitude of leadership is decisive in the long run. There is evidence that this attitude of leadership is growing, it's not getting weaker, it's growing.

So, to avoid having further failures and further frustrations, maybe what we have to do is to attack the problem where it

* Center for Urban Education, *Community Attitudes in Bedford-Stuyvesant: An Area Study* (New York, Summer, 1967).

can be attacked—successfully. You talked in your opening remarks about practical limitations and success strategies. Maybe
we ought to be looking at a success strategy, or a combination
of success strategies, and that means, I think, that we have to
look at a competitive system. I don't think you can create a
full competitive system, but you can create competitive pressures. What you're trying to do in Roxbury, what the storefront
academies do in Harlem, even what Leon Sullivan does with
school dropouts in OIC [Opportunities Industrialization Cen-
ter]—there's a whole variety of competitive strategies. Maybe
the tuition system has done a deal of good. Maybe there is a
way through the competitive system idea to exert some leverage on the existing system. Maybe a strategy to break up the
system is also a strategy that introduces new energies and new
vitality. Maybe we have to look, at least for the large cities,
at decentralization, not just as a means of an assault on a
system that we don't like but really as a means of creating
a new political constituency for the support of putting more
resources into that sector of the system that has been starved,
in order to improve the quality of education for those children
who have been denied.

That, I think, is the most significant political aspect of decentralization—new thousands of people who have never been
concerned before with education are now involved, hence now
making demands, and demands which will have to be responded to. In fact they're being responded to in some ways.
Milton Galamison sits on the Board of Education in New
York City.* A year ago he was president of a rump board, but
now he's a respectable member of a new establishment. The
quality of education, by the way, hasn't improved yet, but
it's not unimportant that thousands of parents now in that

* When the composition of the New York City board was altered by the
1969 school decentralization act, Galamison, as well as other members of
that board, were replaced by borough representatives.

city are so involved that they are beginning to ask the kind of questions middle-class parents have always asked: Why aren't our children being taught better? What is this about reading scores? Parents all over the city are now beginning to learn about reading scores. That is the beginning of a political process, of the development of a political constituency.

My point is that maybe this is not the time to look for structural changes, because they're not possible, but to look at other strategies to stimulate change and in an institution that is going to be with us whether we like it or not.

Clyde Ferguson: A brief comment on that. You say structural change is not possible. I don't think that should be accepted at face value. The problem of developing this new constituency through decentralization seems to me to be imposing on this new constituency, which is primarily black, a white middle-class kind of presupposition of what the structure should be. The fact of the matter has been that the only leverage black people in this country have had has not been through decentralization but has been through a kind of national centralization. Black people are national more than anything else—the leverage that black people have had has come from the fact that they have been able to operate principally on the federal level. Everything that has drifted down has been as a result of that. It seems to me a monstrous error—and I know that there is disagreement—to take decentralization, principally a white middle-class political value, and impose it on a group of people who are organized by the racist system in precisely another way. As a minority they have never been able to operate on the *local* level effectively as a political constituency. But as a large *national* minority they have been able to. Whatever has come out of this system has come from that national push, and I think it's going backwards to go to decentralization. The direction should be exactly the opposite.

One last comment that comes to mind in terms of integration as a goal: I just don't think that you can keep stating that if you get the proper skin mix, as I know your analysis would show, that the quality is automatically going to come. I just can't bring myself to believe that if you have got one hundred black skins that there is something inherent in that particular group which means that you can't have quality education in that particular group. I think in terms of what we're talking about in short range we have to recognize that this is one fact that can't be changed. The question is not whether or not we can get a proper skin mix and still have the same bad education, but whether or not we can get quality education into that particular group that we can't do very much with.

Kenneth Clark: I think that Mike's comment plus Clyde's point up what Harry said: if you take these three objectives it will not necessarily follow that the pursuit of one will not be in conflict with the other. To come back to Mike's point: that decentralization might be more significant in obtaining objective three—quality—and some political leverage for the minority groups in the governance of education in big cities. I don't see that as being contrary to structural change.

By the way, I do think there is a problem in the pursuit of decentralization in trying to deal with one aspect of the problem of education in the big cities, where there is a high concentration of minority groups. But the more successful decentralization is, the greater the chances of intensifying and reinforcing segregation. We worried about this, Jim Allen and the Regents and those of us who had to be for decentralization as an interim thing. We have had to tell ourselves that this is a limited objective, because the centralized system has not only failed in integration, which it did, but it failed even more miserably in doing something about quality—your point three. So, because these children are in school for only one lifetime, we feel that we have to do something now to see that they do not continue to be the human casualties of a criminally inferior system. But I wonder whether this approach will not inevitably deflect us from the very difficult and crucial problem of American racism and education. If we concentrate on the short-range strategy of decentralization, which one has to develop in order to save a child now, at least in the inner cities, it is going to be inimical to racial mix. If we are too ready to make concessions at the expense of solving the fundamental problem of the racist organization of the American education system or nonsystem, we may not be any different from the other practical strategists.

The basic problem as I see it in American education is that we have inherited race as an integral part of the system. To cure some of the more flagrant symptoms we might have to make certain concessions to solving the basic problem, but are we willing to settle for this? Are there not things which we ought to address ourselves to that confront the fundamental problem of trying to rid American education of race?

Franklin Roosevelt: I hope we will get into the area of competition in the education system later on. I throw out a word of warning that we in New York have gone through a very serious referendum, to change our constitution to permit state funds to be more directly used for one of the competitive systems; namely, the various church systems. In taking up competitive systems, you must keep in the back of your mind the very serious church-state issue; I hope we will not get into this.

On the matter of structural change and its effect on attitudes, I think that we have got to be more specific in discussing structural change in the big core cities of New York, Chicago, and Philadelphia, as distinguished from a quite different problem of the smaller but important cities with core problems, such as Rochester and Syracuse. In Rochester a very interesting experiment involving a considerable amount of busing is going on. In New York City this becomes a far more difficult thing to achieve. Rochester is approaching, or beginning to approach—I think, Jim, you would agree—the beginning of a success story in integration.

Also, I think you have to be more specific when we discuss the primary and secondary levels of education, as distinguished from the university, college, and postgraduate levels, because there again the problem is an entirely different one. So we have first the magnitude of the big city as distinguished from the smaller city, and then the level of education that we are talking about. The structural, and therefore, the attitudinal result is entirely different as we discuss these different areas.

Now, to comment on this structural problem, it seems to me that it breaks down into two really quite separate categories. I was fascinated by Dean Ferguson's comparison to and his remarks about the federal level having been far more successful in promoting change. But basically aren't we discussing two different things? What I think the parents in New York City —Dr. Galamison—are really interested in is a voice in the quality of education. Whether it is Intermediate 201 or any other school. They are far less interested—at least for the moment—in the financial budgetary problems related to this. I agree that if we could ever remove the financial problem from the school district and put that into a central area—I would think possibly the state working with the federal government—but leave to the local community the educational problems of the participation of the parents, the setting of the standards of the teachers, and so forth, then local participation and local control—decentralization is the commonly used word —could be readily achieved, whereas the structural change resulting from centralization of the financial responsibility could be achieved if we follow something along the lines Dr.

Allen was talking about. When we talk of structural change, can we be more specific as to what particular part of the system we want to change?

I think that one of the desirable structural changes in higher education would be to relate college students, as, for example, in Columbia University, to a damn good tutorial service in the very Harlem in which Columbia is located, to which they now have no relationship whatsoever. Those kids could be made to feel that they were performing a constructive role. Here again is a voice, crying in the wilderness for participation, that ought to be used. And I think this is true to an extent, also, at Berkeley, and on many many other campuses. Certainly, at Harvard—or, to an extent that other institution known as Yale, which some of us recognize—the university student body could be used in structural change.

Jerome Wiesner: I think Ken is right that we probably want to go to the heart of the problem at some point. But I think the relevance of talking about structural change is that you are not going to do the thing you want without structural change. And I think that the *kind* of change is probably secondary to making change. I think this is why you may say you would like to see the federal government take a stronger hand, and you would like to see the city system busted up. We have the anomaly in Boston of talking about doing both at the same time. We would like to bust up the city system into smaller subsections and at the same time do what Jim's talking about, which is to get a metropolitan educational system. And there are arguments for doing both.

I think the thing to remember is that every management or organizational system gets rigidities, becomes defensive, and then can't be changed. The moment you break the boundaries —no matter how you break them and restructure it—you have set up a situation into which you can now move to do the things you want to do, and eventually it, too, will also have to be changed. Maybe ten years from now in New York City it will seem sensible to go back to a centralized system because efficiency will seem to be more important than academic change and academic performance, which seems to be the important thing at the moment. I don't think there is any absolute in these things. You can defend change as the only way to get people concentrating.

Another thing that change does—somebody said it in terms of bringing thousands of parents in—is to get the professionals excited and involved in a different way. They may see some hope, in contrast to years and years of frustration in a structure that didn't seem willing to move. There are many positive reasons for looking for this kind of change.

Race, Class, Separatism, and Integration

Kenneth Boulding: I have come to the conclusion lately that integration is what I call a diversionary ideal. That is, something which satisfies us because we can work at it and know that it won't be done while in the meantime the real problems tend to go unanswered. I must confess that I am deeply, intensively bored with the subject of race. I think it is the most boring subject in the world. Unfortunately, we have to go on talking about it.

My own hunch is that the main problem in this country is not race at all but class. And we are extremely unwilling to admit this because our ideology says that ours is a classless society. The brute fact is that we ain't. We are a society for the middle class, of the middle class, and by the middle class, and we don't really care much about the lower class. First place, it is so small, only about 20 per cent, if it is *that*. It doesn't have many votes, and it doesn't have much influence, so we run into all sorts of trouble.

Out where I come from—Boulder, Colorado—the Negro is

an all-right chap, on the whole, because he's in the federal government, so he is the middle class. Our problem is the Spanish-speaking American. One of the most dangerous assumptions in this country is that the race problem is a Negro problem. It is, but it is not the only one. It is a great mistake to concentrate on this. In Denver, the Negroes aren't doing too badly. They go to the eleventh grade; so they are increasing their income rapidly. The Spanish-speaking Americans go only to the eighth. The Spanish Americans are going downhill and soon. I suspect that you would find that the real problem in this country is the poor whites. These are just as much a minority group and nobody pays any attention to them. This is the minority group that is going to cause all the trouble, preventing us from doing all these other things we want to do. Nobody pays any attention to them at all.

I must say also that "minority group" is the damndest balderdash I have ever heard. Who isn't a minority group? I grew up in what today would be called a ghetto. I didn't have the slightest idea what it meant.

Talking about attitudes, the main attitude I think we have to change is that of the good liberal white. I must say that I have been observing with a little sadistic pleasure a number of white liberals exhibiting catatonic cultural shock because of the black-power types and the brown-power types—the brown-power types in our part of the country are much more fun than the black-power types. And they go into a catatonic state, and they say you can't mean me. Race has always been supremely unimportant.

I do not know what this committee can say that isn't absolutely scandalous or a cliché. I do think it is time for somebody to say something that has not been said for thirty years. Anything this committee has said has been said for thirty years, and it is a lot of tripe.

If you want the economics of it—it's only the physicists who talk about the economics—one of the major problems in this country, frankly, gentlemen, is that the tax system favors the rich, not the poor. What is even worse is that social welfare is for the rich. Our subsidies go to the rich, our agricultural subsidies go to the rich, our educational subsidies go to the rich —and very little goes to the poor. That is, I think, the awful truth of the matter. Talk about structural change—what we've really got to talk about is structural change of the tax system. We've really got to get rid of the exempt municipals and cheerful things of this sort.

The assumption of the War on Poverty is that you make the poor richer without making the rich poorer. As a mass assumption, very frequently you can. And if you can do this, it is all to the good. On the other hand I have come to the very uncomfortable conclusion that our economic development does not in and of itself really solve the problem of poverty. These economic problems are crucial. I must say I have a great deal of sympathy with the competition jag on this. I think the parallel is, of course, the G.I. Bill of Rights, which was rather good, despite a few fly-by-night schools.

Suppose we do something like this: We go to a voucher plan. You give every child $500 to $1,000 a year, and he can spend it in any way he wants. And give every Negro child $1,500.

Jerome Wiesner: But that's racism.

Kenneth Boulding: But I mean I am in favor of racism. I think racism is important. Well, they call it discrimination—not the same thing as racism at all. These are two quite different subjects. If you want to introduce some kind of counterweight to discrimination, this is where the federal government comes in. We may see the federal government, the whole taxing-and-subsidy business, as a total picture weighted toward correcting some of these ills of society. This seems to me to be its major function.

C. Vann Woodward: We Southerners have tried so many of these things for a long time. One of them was to pretend that racism didn't exist. We tried hard at that, but it didn't work. And boring or not, it comes up again and again. Separate and equal, separate but equal, separate and not equal. We are watching with some detachment, and sometimes dismay, these old debates being repeated up here. And we are, I think, particularly dismayed at the suddenness with which our liberal friends in the North have given up on the integration thing, as I think many of them have. I hope they think it may be desirable as an ultimate goal, but they consider it impracticable, at least in the city. And if it's unfeasible, we must make the best of a bad situation and go along with segregation. Once you get black leadership and white leadership agreed on this business of separate courses and separatism, it looks bad for the cause of integration for a long time to come.

Kenneth Clark: It gives support to the Kerner Commission's description of polarization.

C. Vann Woodward: That was the great argument against integration in the South, that it just wasn't realistic.

Kenneth Clark: Are you saying that the separatism which is now fashionable is unrealistic?

C. Vann Woodward: I hear much talk that integration is impracticable, that as an ultimate goal it is an ideal like equality, but that as a practical program it is unfeasible. I know that this isn't a universal attitude, but I hear more of it, and I am concerned. I think these are the basic things we have to discuss —whether we are headed toward integration or toward quite separate but equal peaceful coexistence in our educational program for the races.

Franklin Roosevelt: I totally understand the new attitude of some of our Negro leadership about separatism, and the frus-

trations that brought them to this attitude. But in my work
in the Equal Employment Opportunity Commission I saw its
effect in employment. I was instrumental in bringing about a
new compact between the big paper companies in the South
and the two unions involved. And it was very clear that there
were two ladders of promotion, the white ladder and the Negro
ladder. The Negro ladder stopped at the level of the shop
foreman and did not reach to the superintendent above that
and on up the ladder to the executive level. I couldn't agree
more with you, Mr. Vann Woodward and Ken, that if we
are going to have what we claim to have, a country which
provides equal opportunity for a nation of equal citizens, if
we are going to have equal economic opportunity, then we
have got to start with an integrated school system. Frankly,
Mr. Boulding, I think that if we can start with an integrated
school system we will deal a deathblow to subsequent discrim-
inations. I agree with you that they are different subjects, but
they are closely related.

James Allen: We are really raising a question here of whether
integration should be both a long- and a short-range goal,
either one, or no goal at all.

Eugene Patterson: Well, I want to agree with my fellow
Southerner, Professor Woodward, that we do detect a certain
wavering among blacks and whites in this country, generally,
on the whole subject of integration. Is it a priority, or have we
not in fact already accepted the Kerner Commission polarization? And perhaps the Southerner looks at this with the detachment that Professor Woodward mentions because we have
been through an extension of what Mr. Roosevelt said for the
last decade in the South—a living example that you can move
attitudes with a little centralized power behind the effort.
Structural change, if you will. A decade ago in the city of
Atlanta everything was segregated—buses, picture shows, pub-

lic auditoriums, restaurants—now everything is desegregated. But we are now falling heir to the Northern problem, and there's no blinking that fact.

Our moderator knows this problem better than any of us at the table, and I'd like to pose a question to him.

Atlanta now is facing a flight to the suburbs like that in Detroit or Cleveland or New York or Washington, D.C. Our rural areas astonished me with the ease with which they were able to integrate. After all the years of being told by their politicians that this was impossible, they did it! And now you'll find salt and pepper football teams and bands and student bodies all over rural Georgia, perhaps integrating with more ease than you now find in our big urban areas, which are generally Northern.

But in talking about structural change, even Dr. Allen's idea—which on its face appears a good one, to centralize the financing of schools in the state and federal treasuries, and remove the power of the purse from the local man—even this will be popular in the South. We have this already in Georgia; a tax-revision committee has suggested this not in an effort at social advance but in an effort of political popularity. The local property taxpayer wants out. They want to put it on the state, you see, because to this point, there are no federal programs that are truly meaningful for the big budget of a public school. We now have a debate going on about the economics of it—not the social applications. They want to add one per cent to the sales tax and let the state finance the schools. Unfortunately, this only comes out to $90 million a year, and localities now are providing $150 million a year. There is a slight gap there.

My question to you, Mr. Howe, in looking at these structural changes from a more centralized point of view: What truly would happen, from your experience, if the state and above all, of course, in application to the South, if the federal

treasury began running the public schools financially and re-
lieving the locality of the taxing duty? What then would happen so far as the Negro child is concerned in the schools of
the country? Would this really have an effect on social develop-
ments and, from your experience, wouldn't you find Congress
still reflecting that local attitude just as effectively as the
localities now do it, if not more so?

Harold Howe: Well, different things would happen in different states. You now have a number of states which run a
centralized financing system for their schools: Delaware, for
example; Hawaii another. But you've got a very different
position in your chief state school officer in the South and in
the position that Jim Allen found himself in, in New York
State. First, that official in the South is elected politically and
he's got to *get* himself elected. If you did entirely centralize
the disbursement of funds in the state, and therefore leverage
over school organization and over the question of who goes to
school with whom, a person who depends on political election
will be at the core of that. Until such time as he can convince
a reasonable portion of the electorate that some change makes
sense in current practices, he is very likely to become a brake
on the system rather than an element of change.

Eugene Patterson: And certainly in the South now you would
find this system electing segregationist governors and breeding
resistance to the federal effort. Would this be a Southern
phenomenon only, or would this be extensive in the country?

Harold Howe: No, not only Southern. There are elected chief
state school officers, to use that simple fact, in a number of
other places—Montana, Indiana, and so on. But I think that
this kind of a change would bring some elements of leverage in
some states where there *are* big cities. This has to be done at
the state level in those states where it will make a difference

of a positive kind. But for the federal government to try to enter into this and say that all states must in some fashion do this in order to receive federal largess, I think might well set things back in more than half of the states.

Eugene Patterson: Of course, right now some forty counties in my state simply dispense with federal aid rather than desegregate the schools.

Eli Ginzberg: Can I go back to Ken's statement and say that he has been trying to get us, I think, to deal with the racial facets of the educational system. I do think that Boulding is right when he argues that this race-and-class thing ought to be at least looked at together as a minimum requirement. I don't want to dissolve race, but I sure want to look at it together with class.

The first point is that there is a constant, continuing, and very important racist factor in the allocation of funds for education in the United States. Period. Number One. It occurs between North and South and between central city and suburb. It has a class element to it, also, because the South is poor, but race is fundamental.

Number Two is that the leadership of the educational establishment has never been committed to and is not even at this late date commited to educating both poor people and Negro and Mexican-American people. They again overlap. That is, it is basically as my colleague professor, Dr. [John] Fischer of Teachers College [Columbia University] keeps saying: the public school has been very successful in educating middle-class kids, by and large. It has never really faced the challenge of and done a good job with black kids, Mexican-American kids, or poor white kids. They get just the same bad deal. So that the establishment has not yet put a high priority delivery on that front.

The third thing is that we haven't, even at this late stage, experimented enough or haven't really any sense of how to construct a curriculum and to deliver effective education to either poor kids or Negro kids. We simply don't have what it takes. It's obviously do-able, as far as I'm concerned, but the whole system is not really sensitized to doing it and does not do it very well.

The fourth point is that we completely ignore and refuse to take remedial action on the malperformance of the system. Many times I have thought what was going to happen to the Commissioner of New York if somebody brought a case in the courts stating that you're obligated to teach these kids. The state has the responsibility to do that. And the state simply does not meet its constitutional commitments. Suppose you do it in the United States.

Kenneth Clark: I was going to say that such a suit is in preparation now.

Eli Ginzberg: Is it? I always wanted to introduce it. You know, in the Swiss cantons I gather that if a youngster shows up for military service and he's not adjudged to be mentally deficient and he still doesn't pass the examination, they ship him back to the canton and say bring him up to educational standards. You just keep sending him back home until they deliver.

We have had unequivocal evidence from military data for a very long time that 60 to 70 percent of the Negroes in the poor parts of the United States do not pass an eighth-grade equivalency examination. But there are no implementing devices here, no automatic devices, compensatory devices to say, What the hell is going on here—you can't get away with that! You just can't get away with that! You better do something this time. You cannot go in two directions simultaneously, except tactically. Strategically, you have to decide that you are in favor of desegregation and integration or you'll get into murderous troubles in this country. It's part of a larger effective package of getting the country to run right. While it's true that, tactically, you may want to desegregate schools, you have to improve black schools for a long while, for they are going to remain black for a long while. We understand that. But the central commitment has to be in terms of moving toward a desegregated society.

The only other comment I want to make is that I was very taken with Mr. Roosevelt's comment about the manpower implication of better schooling, but I don't see much change that new construction acts—even $5 billion of federal funds a year—really deliver for the poor people and the Negro kids in schools. The only chance that I see is to take college juniors and seniors and graduate students and ask them to go into those schools on a one-year basis. Leave the bureaucracy alone, because they don't want to be touched, and do a teaching job alongside of them. Just alongside of them, because you're not going to break this system; you're not going really to be able to change the system by new money. The only chance that I think you have is if you don't frighten the bureaucrats. And if you put these kids who are enthusiastic and who believe that Negro kids can be taught into the schools—if you put them in for enough years—I think you have a fair chance, then. It would be good for the youngsters who one of these days won't have to be killed anymore in Vietnam.

Jerome Wiesner: I think you *should* frighten the bureaucrats.

Eli Ginzberg: You should what?

Jerome Wiesner: You should frighten the bureaucrats.

Franklin Roosevelt: I think, also, that while some of the schools have gone to teachers' training programs, by and large there is relatively little field training specifically for teachers who are going to go into schools which we have to face are going to continue to be primarily Puerto Rican or Negro or Mexican-American or Indian schools or poor white schools. More field training should be added to the professional teachers' curriculum. If you add to that this wave of young people who I think are dying to get into the act, we might have some drastic results rather quickly.

ALLOCATION OF FUNDS AND REWARD SYSTEMS
RELATED TO PERFORMANCE

Harold Howe: Your statement, Mr. Ginzberg, about allocation of funds being racist can be addressed to two levels of government in terms of the distribution formulas states use for allocating state funds to public schools. I think there is very good evidence that the big cities are being short-changed in that process in many states. There have been some improvements made in New York State, Jim, in this regard. But we're still a long way off, and in many states cities have a dramatically low level of support compared to the suburbs. There is definite recommendation for changing these formulas.

There's the clear possibility of seeking equalization-type grants at the federal level. This has been explored. Somewhere among those many plans there is a possibility of an allocation system that sets the floor, at least from the federal level, for education and a differential type of grant to different states.

On the leadership point that you made, here again I agree about the leadership of the educational establishment not being committed to the poor; I do detect some change. It's on their agenda. It was not on their agenda four years ago. They don't know—but this leads directly to your third point—they don't know what to do about it.

Kenneth Clark: And what they are doing involves palliatives, really.

Harold Howe: Let me say there, Ken, that, in many discussions on this exact problem, the only positive suggestion we get is that we need to produce just as rapidly as possible some successful models. That these need to be, if necessary, models which use Jerry Wiesner's suggestion for competitive arrangements. Maybe they can be built into school systems in some cases; maybe they're newly started enterprises in others. But they need to be large enough scale models so they aren't just an individual school somewhere but, rather, a city. I'd like to see this group suggest the possibility that funds be made available to selected cities to create these models, and at least in a proportion of a third or a half of the educational system in the city, and let this model compete, win over the other half—or something of that kind. There is nothing like that going on.

I won't comment on Jim's ignoring the malperformance of the system. But I quite agree we can't go in two directions, your final point, although in the federal government we find ourselves in a real dilemma about how much emphasis you put on the integration matter, while you realize that for years to come there will be definite segregated blocks in the city.

Eli Ginzberg: Could I make a suggestion? Could you use a certificate from the commissioner, the state commissioner of education, which would not permit the erection of any new school or the expansion of any existing school except under certain criteria which would contribute to or detract from integration? We do that now with hospitals in New York State. You cannot build any new hospital or expand any hospital in New York State unless you meet certain socially determined criteria on the constitutional structure.

James Allen: We can do something about that now. It depends on how far we go, because in the next session of the Legislature, they will take the authority away from us. But at the present time we have certain funds that we can refuse to allocate unless there is an integration component in the development of the school or in the consolidation of the district, and so on. But it's limited. There are a lot of things we try to do and push to do, but a person in my position has the responsibility of pushing forward in the direction you want to go as far as you can but not so far as to get legislation passed. Every year in the New York State Legislature there is a bill that says they're going to take my powers away. Last year it had eighty signers on it, almost half the Legislature. You play this political game. How far can you go and what do you do with the Legislature? I think we make progress, but . . .

Christopher Edley: I'd like to throw in an idea, in the context of what Professor Ginzberg has said, that has been kicking around for some time. I think that the Regents system in New York theoretically gets at it, but doesn't quite succeed. That is the parallel of private enterprise. I don't think the military system is a good parallel. I think that the Department of Defense has certain advantages, but these are the advantages that result from copying something from the private-enterprise system. There's a hardheadedness in the approach which gives specific men the responsibility for achieving certain objectives. There are penalties built in if they don't succeed. So, the company commander must train his company up to a certain level of efficiency or his record suffers as a result. I think that we should stop for a moment and consider how the parallel of private enterprise could be applied to the school system, and it could be expected to produce a finished product at the end of high school. The kids can all compete with each other. For simplicity, let's say we're striving to turn out a fungible item. Now if we put into the educational system the bonuses, the premium pay, the result orientations, the values on the quality of the product turned out, we are immediately given certain yardsticks for measuring the results, which, I believe, would accomplish most of what we are trying to say should be done in the school system.

To be specific, let me apply it to Professor Ginzberg's five points. I'll skip the first one, allocation of funds, because that's difficult. The mission of educational leadership. Well, the superintendent of education, the principal of the public school system, and his assistants will all be penalized monetarily. People in private industry are not only working for their salaries, they're also working for the glory that comes from knowing that they are building, knowing that they are producing and turning out. That should be so in the educational system. This leadership could be reoriented in this harsh fashion, I contend, to a result orientation in dealing with ghetto youth and all other people in the system: the technical ability to teach the poor. You could have a school principal whose own income and livelihood and tenure turn on how successful the teachers are in teaching his clientele, his raw material. The assistant principals would do whatever they could to coach, to instruct the teachers on how to instruct better. Everybody's salary above the line would turn on whether or not the result is satisfactory.

On the remedies of the malfunction of the system, I think we have to emphasize the fact that there hasn't been a breakthrough on technical educational knowledge, the psychology necessary to reach these ghetto youths. But I, for one, have faith in the ability of the teacher to instruct if given the right incentive. I don't think the problem is whether or not a teacher in a classroom can get through to the ghetto kid; the teacher obviously can get through to the ghetto kid if the teacher's motivation is high enough, if the teacher has the motivation for staying after school to work with difficult kids without pay but knowing that there is a bonus or some reward at the end.

Jerome Wiesner: Did *your* teachers have a bonus coming?

Christopher Edley: No. I came from a segregated school system, but there the teachers had the enjoyment of seeing their students go on to the best colleges. If these students could come from a small Southern town and get into the prestigious schools, this was a reward factor for the teachers involved.

It's my contention that if we zero in on the practical problem, which is teaching my child and teaching the ghetto child to be competitive, to have the competitive edge necessary in this society today, these other objectives and problems will fade away.

One final comment that gets beyond Professor Ginzberg's remarks. I cannot agree with you on the role of volunteers. I don't think the system can turn on whether or not we can bring in these additional inputs. The system has to succeed or fail on our ability to take what is in the system now and make it function and function effectively. I am certainly in favor of some structural changes. There is a more fundamental way of getting at the problem, and that is how to make the teacher who is in the classroom today a more effective teacher.

Franklin Roosevelt: I agree.

Christopher Edley: I think that in trying to rely on the idealism of this teacher, we must not deny the fact that this teacher is interested in tenure, security, and income; we must use all of those things. I think we have to face up to the fact that the present structure gives the teacher automatic tenure in terms of the length of service without seemingly caring one iota whether or not this teacher has the ability to reach the child. I am saying in essence that this education business is a hard business, and education is so important today that we must look at it in a competitive entrepreneurial fashion. The ghetto kid goes to the school system to get an education. Everybody goes to the school system to get an education. It is the school system's job to reach that kid. If we can't do it in the present structure—and we're not doing it in the present structure— I am suggesting that we might be able to change the structure.

Kenneth Clark: Changing the reward system?

Christopher Edley: Changing the reward system so that an inefficient teacher can be fired or given lower pay than a master teacher or a teacher who is able to reach the kid so that the kid can pass the Regents examination, so the kid can get admitted to college, so the kid can qualify for a job when coming out of vocational school—there are many standards that can be used. But the point is that the standards are result-oriented. Whatever it is that we want for our children. You want your children to have love of learning, fine. But it is my contention that the ghetto kid can't afford love of learning. The ghetto kid needs certain skills and knowledge which will enable him to make his way through life.

Harold Howe: I think we need to discuss this point at considerable length. I, superficially, would say that it's worth pursuing. You ought to impose it on the colleges and universities at the same time. You shouldn't let these professors get away with inefficiencies either. So let's assume that it's an across-the-board suggestion rather than just a narrow one imposed on the schools.

Harry Rowen: I think Mr. Edley is pushing in exactly the right direction. And I would like to ask you a question about a specific scheme which would do a lot of these things. It's not original, but I'm curious to get expert comment—not on the political feasibility, which I am sure is very tough, but simply on the performance if it were politically feasible. Take New York City. Suppose the school board were to contract with private schools, either existing or newly established, to do the following: to produce results measured by achievement tests, skills, measurable skills of the kind that are very widely used and can be assessed in a more or less objective fashion by an independent entity, with possibly the wrinkle that if the school exceeds the target, it gets a bonus; and if it falls short of the target, it gets docked from the contracted amount. And the contract is to produce results. To produce achievement, so measured. Would it work?

Jerome Wiesner: Oh, I don't think it would really quite work.

Harry Rowen: Well, there are lots of variants, particular vouchers going to particular individuals, and so on. Would something like that work?

Jerome Wiesner: In something like what we are talking about, the voting is essentially done by the parents.

Harry Rowen: Look, would people address my proposal first, would it work?

Unidentified: Yes.

Harry Rowen: I am not asking for political feasibility. I am saying, assuming that it could be accepted, would these private institutions be able to produce . . .

Harold Howe: I think it would be most useful to have somebody who's a little bit of a specialist in human development and the way individuals change and grow and the different rates and the problems of expectations of them at different times in their life, and this kind of thing, comment on this. I don't know who is exactly the party to do it, but Dr. Erikson might want to say a word or two about whether the expectation of standards that is implied in this sort of suggestion is something that you can transfer from producing TV sets that measure up to producing people that measure up, or whether there are real problems here.

Erik Erikson: First, let me say my colleague Pettigrew somewhat undercut my position by saying that attitude changes could be primarily brought about by structural change. This is, of course, correct when you speak of the child. The question is, What is the motivation? Where do you get the motivation for structural change, and where do you get the people to man the new structures when they are formed?

Now about the achievement, I think what has gone through the whole discussion is this double view of ours about achieving especially according to certain tests. I wish Tom Pettigrew would say some more, because he has written about it, and obviously it has done a great deal of harm. Why doesn't one look at the tests and how they were made; on whom they were standardized?

Mitchell Sviridoff: If you accept the tests, accept them for the moment, there is some evidence that under very special circumstances, some of the schools have been able to teach. Ken knows of a few schools in Harlem, like you do, where many scores are up to par. The Workers Defense League experience in preparing ghetto kids, many of them school dropouts, to compete in apprentice examinations is another example. And it is doing it in a very short time. As a matter of fact it even prepared them to compete for the Foreign Service Officer's Examination with some degree of success.

But if you look at why these few work, you find very special characteristics. The first thing you find is a very special leader, the principal. And then you find that that special leader attracts very special teachers. And you don't find that they do anything very unusual in the school. There are no new techniques; they're teaching in a rather traditional way. But there is a certain air of electricity in that school or in that Workers Defense League setting that makes a difference. So the answer to your question, would it work—yes, with the right leader who would attract the right teachers and the right circumstances, the chances are it would work. And therefore it would be a very desirable thing to do. It would not say, however, that the whole school system is capable of doing this. But I think it would have a very jarring effect on the system.

Jerome Wiesner: What Mike says is true though. Under any circumstances, wherever you can get a good principal and a bunch of good teachers, whether it is in the New York City school system or in a private school, education will work. The whole question is how to break through the system. After the teachers have been there a while, many lose their enthusiasm, many principals lose their enthusiasm. The whole thing degenerates.

Kenneth Clark: Similar teachers and principals apparently don't lose their enthusiasm in the suburbs.

Jerome Wiesner: That's right. This is why you want to get at the structure.

Harold Howe: In the suburbs you have a high level of participation by community people who insist that these teachers do their job. They bore in all the time. I used to be superintendent of the Scarsdale school system.

Kenneth Clark: What is built into the suburban system is what Chris and Harry are asking to build into an urban or urban-poor system. Actually, the suburban system is very high on penalties and rewards, or penalties for inefficiency and rewards for efficiency, as you know.

Clyde Ferguson: It's very high. It's how many kids out of this high school get admitted to college. That's where the rewards come—which colleges they get admitted to. The school that produces is the school that gets the resources, and that's where the malallocation comes in. You get a city like Newark. In Weequahic High School we have the teachers who produce the kids who get admitted to colleges. They get all the new resources, they get all the new curriculum innovations. The other schools go down the drain because the system doesn't reward them. The system says, If your kids don't go to college, then you're the junk pile. Consequently a teacher who is enthusiastic starts in the school and finds out he's on a dead end. So he goes to Weequahic.

Christopher Edley: We don't have to speculate. We have an ex-Scarsdale principal. How important, after the college en-

trance exam, to you and your faculty was the question of how
many more students or how fewer students you got into the
Ivy League colleges and to the other prestigious schools? Was
pride in the school based on this? What was the source of this
pride? Was it pressure from the parents, the upper-middle-
class and upper-class parents who had children in that school?
I think you could enlighten us a bit on this.

Harold Howe: Well, there was a real dualism toward this sort
of thing. In communities like Scarsdale, it is a source of pride
that this payoff exists in terms of future educational opportunities. But there is also the other side of the coin. This high
expectation and the pressures to achieve it are destructive to
a fair proportion of young people and result in all kinds of
nonsuccess. Programs that are too much for the youngster
may lead to everything—even suicide. What worries me is the
idea of any kind of single expectation. I think that human
beings are different enough so that expectations for certain
levels of performance to some degree must be defined in terms
of working with the individual being.

Christopher Edley: How do you keep the drones in the system
from using that as a defense for lack of performance?

Harold Howe: That is a very real problem. And I think Ken
Clark has been one of the great spokesmen on trying to get
across the point that the central city schools need to have
high expectations for the youngsters there. This has been one
of the major points in your writings, Ken. I think it has been
a great contribution. There has been too much excuse made,
just as you imply, that "these youngsters" come from "these
kinds of families." How can you expect them to learn? They
don't expect them to learn, so they don't learn.

There was a very interesting experiment in California.*

* Robert Rosenthal and Lenore Jacobson, *Pygmalion in the Classroom:
Teacher Expectation and Pupils' Intellectual Development* (New York,
Holt, Rinehart, and Winston, 1968), 240 pages.

Teachers were told that a particular group of youngsters, who actually had average or below-average IQ's, had very high IQ's, and this misinformation resulted in high performance from this group. The teachers apparently registered a high expectation in their work with these youngsters. By God, this guy ought to perform, let's make him—and he did! Well, there is some lesson in that sort of thing.

Eli Ginzberg: I don't think we should let it go that easily. I think you've got to make the explicit statement that a white racist America was not interested in good performance and in fact encouraged a low one. You've got to make it explicit because it meant that, throughout the South, and in the North, the basic established classes were not interested in "spoiling farm hands by getting them too well educated." And as recently as last year, the superintendent of schools in a Texas city said, "Why after all, what do you expect but that a lot of kids are going to drop out of high school? We can't have a whole country full of geniuses with everybody going on to college!" This is the racist aspect of the problem.

Jerome Wiesner: It's deeper that that. Several years ago I was on the local school committee, where the most shocking things happened to me. There was a discussion of a man they wanted to hire to handle a seventh grade in a poor white section of town. This guy had had mostly D's and E's at Cornell; it wasn't quite certain how he had graduated. Now I said, "What the hell are you hiring that stupid man for to handle this class?"

They said, "That's the trouble with you people that got too much education. You don't realize that a man who has had trouble learning might have a better chance in dealing with these kids than someone who has been highly educated."

All right. But this guy, as it turned out, had been a football player; he was six foot two, and he was going to be able to manage the discipline. All they gave a damn about in this white suburban community was getting those kids to the point at which they no longer had to hold them in school. They weren't planning on teaching them anything and this teacher wasn't capable of teaching it. I think you'll find more of this in the school system of Boston than you'll find in Watertown, Massachusetts, which is a suburb, but it's not absent in the suburbs. If you think that everything's perfect in the suburbs, you're crazy.

IGNORANCE, INTEGRATION, AND IDENTITY

Kenneth Clark: I've been listening to the discussion since Harry's three points and Eli's five points. It seems that most of the discussion is centered on the points two and three: the structural changes which took a great deal of our time, earlier, and the improvement of quality of education. And, here, we again concentrated most of our attention on the more obvious problem of the blatantly inferior quality of education for lower-status children. Ken Boulding tried to broaden our perspective to include various kinds of lower-status kids, poor whites, Mexican-Americans, Negroes; and it certainly is important. But it does seem interesting that we have skirted—except for an occasional casual statement—the problem of basic racist attitudes which undergird all of this.

You know, the structure of education in America is, as we said earlier, a reflection of certain racist assumptions, which, I presume, are a carryover from earlier class assumptions in Europe and elsewhere. The quality problem, someone has said recently, is actually the inferior quality and performance in education for lower-status children, reflecting racist realities and expectations and the use of the educational system to perpetuate this reality.

Now we come back to looking at our primary concern for this conference—what, if anything, can be done about this?

Here it seems to me that we have to look at higher education, because certainly all educational personnel are products of higher education. There must be something about the higher educational process which, if not totally responsible for this, certainly has not helped much—specifically, teacher training. Although I wouldn't want us to blame it all on teacher training in higher educational institutions, because it, too, may simply reflect the same indifference or insensitivity to racism as we see elsewhere. If we look, for example, at the problem of teacher expectations in the inner-city schools and at teacher expectations and performance in the suburbs, I don't see how we can avoid coming to the conclusion that teachers, who are supposed to be professionals with confidence in the potential of human beings, are deficient in areas in which higher education is supposed to provide knowledge. In some research among teachers selected by their principals to discuss teaching with us, the common denominator, interestingly enough true of Negro teachers as well as white teachers, was a profound illiteracy on what you would consider critical areas of knowledge. I mean the attitudes, well not just the attitudes, but the knowledge of cultural anthropology or modern and contemporary knowledge about race and racial differences and racial potentialities, or social psychology. These teachers were primitive in what they said and felt about human beings in terms of race. It would be easy to blame these teachers, but every one of them had a bachelor's degree, and many of them had graduate degrees. They were really illiterate, however, in areas of social science that were relevant to their jobs. I use that as our bridge to the very core problem of the responsibility of institutions of higher education, in general, and specifically on this issue of racism in American education. Our teachers, in very fundamental areas in which they are to function, are ill prepared, no different from the general population in their knowledge, not to mention their attitudes. I can conceive of our changing fiscal arrangements, changing structure, but if you have ignorant people teaching you, there is a question of how much range you have.

Harold Howe: Well, only a small percentage of higher education is involved with teacher training. I'd like to ask Mr. Ogilvie—who, incidentally, was part of a conference at Yale that addressed broadly the general problem of racial issues in higher education both on the curricular and admission sides and in a number of other areas—to add some comments to this one that has been made about teacher-training aspects.

Donald Ogilvie: This thing, this integrationist ethic that everyone seems to share, it disturbs me that we have settled seemingly so easily on the priority of integration as a goal in educational policy-making. From our point of view as black students, the proper priority seems to be educating black people—though this does not necessarily preclude integration. Indeed the relevance of integration to our considerations is its occasional role as a means of achieving quality education rather than its being an end in itself. The necessity is to provide an alternative approach to education in order to get away from the existing system, a process of education, a means of education that would deal with subject matter in such a way that students would see some relevance in it. That it would make sense. That it would actually appear to be worth the effort. It's surprising for some to realize that one can teach black math. The key is to bring the student to approach his subject matter, whether it be mathematics, science, or any other subject, from the context of a black boy or girl who sees the world within a certain framework and says, Well I have to get these skills to do things. We're talking about giving people skills. This is not to say I reject what you were saying about giving black youth a competitive attitude. However, the first order of business is to at least give them the skills which will allow them to compete if and in whatever areas *they* see fit. You can't do this, I contend, if you continue to determine educational policy on the basis of the integrationist ethic, if you continue to talk about the primacy of the goal of integration on the one hand and then depart from there to addressing pragmatically the problem of actually educating black youth.

If you look at education in the university you will see that for many black students, it has been a process of languishing and pushing one's way through and getting on the treadmill and doing one's little step, until, if one is lucky, one stumbles across some things that one can make relevant to understanding one's own experience, the black experience, one's own prospects, black people's prospects. Here you talk about the teacher who has electricity. I say great; that teacher is going to be very effective. But as has also been admitted, there are very few teachers like that. You talked about students dying to get into education. I would offer that they are also getting into education to avoid dying. Their motivation is ideological commitment against the war, but they also just don't feel like casually giving up quite yet, and you know I go along with that. However, they are coming into education with inadequate tools. They are throwing themselves into a situation with children, especially in primary grades, who have about as much knowledge of history of peoples, culture of peoples, the social sciences dealing with interactions between peoples as some of these teachers do. Which is to say, no one in that classroom is equipped to impart any information. As a result new teachers will perpetuate, in effect, the miseducation that exists in America now.

American education from your history text or any other text that occasionally refers to a man or a woman of African descent, basically lies about him most of the time—either by being intent on lying about him in order to establish or prolong a stereotype, or through ignorance. I think the most insidious danger is the ignorance, especially in the historical realm, where the true role of the black man was completely overlooked, hidden, lost. The efforts being made now to correct this are long overdue, and they're not reaching enough people. And the old textbooks are still in the schools. If the textbooks are removed and something more innocuous is placed there, the teacher doesn't know where to fill in the gaps. He hasn't been exposed to the material himself. It's almost as if, in addition to establishing perhaps a training institute sensitizing teachers to the difficulties of the children they're dealing with and the particular situation of the community into which they're going to enter, you would have also to provide them with certain basic information they have missed in their own education. These teachers just do not know, much as our white classmates do not know, much as we black students would not have known had not some of us out of pique, some of us out of anger, some of us out of chance happened to cross a book here or there, or heard a story or gone to the Muslim Mosque, had not we been challenged to go look a little further, find things out ourselves, and check things as they are.

I, again, am upset by the seeming priority placed on integration as such, as a goal. If we're talking about better education for blacks, maybe we should just play down a little bit this ideological binge on integration. You have to remember that black youth hearing "integration" are perhaps not thinking about it in quite as sophisticated terms as you are, that for them integration may still mean that white is right, that they are to strive to be white; that integration means that there is not a black history course taught, because of course that would surely lead to racial isolation, separatism, segregation. If you want to look at emphasis on black studies that way, it is very convenient to do so, but you could also look at it as seeking to comprehend the story of a segment of humanity, keeping it as a segment, but realizing it's a segment that's been ignored. So,

young black people, since this is you, let's look at it; and white
kids, since these are the guys you threw rocks at last weekend
and who beat you with a pipe, let's look at it. Black youth in
the junior high schools and high schools demand black history
courses; they may not really know what they are going to get
out of it, but they do know it's got to be better than what
they're getting now. You do have to admit that a prevailing
cultural particularism does exist and that it has stifled many
black students in and out of the classroom. The need for a
counterbalance is plain. That this need is perceived by students
is obvious. That most teachers and texts are grossly unprepared
presently to meet this need is evident. That working with teachers, texts, and curricula to meet this need can mean significant
improvement in the educational achievement and motivation
of black students has been demonstrated. It remains for you to
approach this issue honestly and constructively. Just by saying
yes, we should have integration, this is our main thing, you're
perhaps doing yourselves, not to mention future generations of
students, a great disservice. Integration is going to be if people
approach each other as enlightened individuals—enlightened
because they know who they are and what they want and what
they are about.

You cannot afford to become so idealistic, and I don't say
this demeaningly at all, that you are afraid to talk about integration as secondary to something else because that would
mean you are running away from it. Let's put it in terms of
integration being your religion. In order to exercise your religion, in order to make it meaningful and real in this life, you
have to enable people to know themselves and the real world.
We are talking about racism, about black youth and white kids
—you must have black children know who they are, and more-
over white children know who they are, because they don't.
White children, as white adults, have been victimized by that
same chauvinistic education that has poisoned the minds of

blacks. Let's get them to know who they are, and black children to know who they are. Perhaps then they can relate to one
another in some better way than we can relate to each other
now. On the university level this means perhaps broadening
course offerings, offering new courses coordinated into directed
programs of study, and conscientious re-evaluation of the adequacy and accuracy of what is presently offered as history,
social science, and literature, in which often much image-
building is based—not only because of the situation that faces
us now, but also because there is viable intellectual material
that has been ignored. And again, truth helps put the world
in a perspective that allows aspiration and achievement to become more than mere words.

Did any of you see the Cosby thing?* How many of you
thought that perhaps those four-year-old children could pick
up that new math not just because that guy was magnetic, but
because it was also related to that other training—that they
were Afro-Americans, that they were black and beautiful children who had a future in life—and they could see that as this
black and beautiful me, my future is to learn this math, and
to learn whatever else this teacher is giving me because obviously it means I'm going to be a better person. I'll be as good
as I should be.

Erik Erikson: I would like to say something about the white
side of this. When I read the education section of the Kerner
Report, I got stuck on the first sentence, which said that American education has been highly successful for the vast majority,
but unsuccessful for some minorities. Now, I find it difficult to
accept such a statement if one considers what we now know
has been overlooked in white education. For example, American education makes it absolutely necessary, I think, to foster

* Bill Cosby, narrator, "Of Black America: Black History: Lost, Stolen
or Strayed?" on CBS television.

more or less conscious prejudices, because in order to have a certain achievement idea, you must have a group of people whom you can keep outside so that you can maintain your so-called higher standards. One has to recognize that a great deal of what we now consider a successful education simply isn't. It isn't successful from the point of view of a human identity, an American identity, since that word was mentioned. For example, American education has been able over all of these decades and centuries to maintain a picture of a happy, successful, well-adjusted American. One might even come to the conclusion that he had to overlook any contrary evidence in order to maintain his own image. It isn't just a matter of the blacks learning who they are, but also, as you said, the whites learning what they are, namely people who need segregation for their own image. It's the *students* now who are convinced they did not get a good education. The good students very often. It is true that new structures have to be built so that attitudes will change for children. But then, it takes a new attitude—and a revolutionary attitude—even to invent the structure and to support it. That's what we have to talk about too.

Bruno Bitker: Some of you here at this table participated in a White House conference on international cooperation, a conference to end all conferences. Five thousand people participated! I presided at the panel on human rights and out of that came the proposal which has led eventually to the President's creation of this President's Commission for the Observance of Human Rights Year and, actually, what brings us to this conference today.

When I first got to thinking about the United States carrying out the proposal from the United Nations that this be the United Nations Human Rights Year, I finally became persuaded that the way to do this was through the world of

education. Then I discovered that the world of education is
the most departmentalized, most fragmented, most sectional-
ized industry in the country. I am a lawyer from out in the
sticks in Milwaukee, and I just knew nothing about this world
of education, but I did finally discover that no matter which
member of the NEA you were talking to, or whether you were
talking to a state agency or a federal agency, everybody was
for human rights. And when Dr. Boulding says there's nothing
new in this in thirty years, I'm persuaded that he's absolutely
right. Everything has been said on the subject. I began to try
to find out what had been written. Well, as all of you know,
the bibliographies are feet, nay miles, long!

I am finally persuaded that the world of education is for
civil rights. But the public is against it. When I first began to
read Dr. Clark's agenda, I came to his second question: "Can
education in a democracy be supported when it seeks to coun-
ter the racial superstitions, irrational theories, hatreds, and
provincialisms of that society?" How do you do it? I hope with
all the brains around this country, around this table, we can
come up with some specific notions not how to train the teachers better, because to do that you have to go back to the public
for the money. And to get bond issues you've got to educate
the public, and you've got to educate them in a very simple,
basic American principle, so basic that it's beyond me, today,
to understand why it's unaccepted. And that is that all men
are created free and equal. You've got to sell this. And you've
got to sell it exactly as you would sell cigarettes.

Erik Erikson: Which you shouldn't in the first place.

Unidentified: Instead of selling cigarettes.

Bruno Bitker: If in this country today, with all of the apparent
information available as to what cigarettes are doing to the
health of the American public, cigarette companies can still

sell *more* cigarettes, there ought to be some way in which we can sell the basic American principle that all men are created free and equal. In the city of Milwaukee, four years ago Mr. [George] Wallace got one of the biggest votes anybody could imagine. Why did he get it? He got it on the very simple basis that all people did not believe that all people were created equal. How do we persuade the American public of their own American principle? When you finally do that, Mr. Commissioner from New York, you aren't going to have to worry about the bill that's introduced in the state legislature every year. It would be laughed down. I hope we devote our time and attention to solving that problem.

Harold Howe: Every school child in the United States probably repeats the oath of allegiance to the flag about being free and equal once a week, if not once a day, and this does not have any results.

Eli Ginzberg: I don't believe this is an American principle. It is only a statement which has never been understood. In terms of policy, unless we get curricula that are really more realistic—which means primarily more history writing that's *real,* not make-believe history writing, and more social science that's *real* and not make-believe—we will not be able to do very much with the community. I can say as an amateur historian that it's just unbelievable what the whites don't know about *white* history, let alone Negro history. There must be curriculum revision, with scholarship broadened and deepened at the collegiate and university level.

The second problem is that Negroes cannot make a contribution to the white community unless a larger proportion of them are represented in important posts. This brings up the system of certification at every level, from getting a job as a garbageman in California, for which you need a high school diploma, all the way up to getting appointed to MIT, Harvard, or Columbia.

Harold Howe: This is the whole problem of credentials.

Eli Ginzberg: Twenty-four to forty-eight hours before Columbia blew up, I was at a meeting with President Kirk and some distinguished rectors from France, discussing how a large university lives effectively in a large urban community. I said to Kirk, nothing's going to happen at this university to change its racist quality, unless you really decide to get some Negro faculty, and I'll tell you how to do it. You go to the Trustees and get from them one additional professorial chair for each of the twenty-two departments. Then you go to the department, and you say that you have twelve months to pick the best guy you can find, and we will trust you on whatever decision you come to. We don't care what the hell the certification is. I said if you get twenty-five new Negro professors around this campus, maybe other places will start to figure out how to do some things, and we'll be going. I said that's do-able. One has to begin with the faculty because whites will never understand except by interchange.

The third one we're doing a little bit better on than most places—and that's why Columbia blew, in part—and that is to do something about bringing Negro students in. It's not enough, but it's happening. Especially at the key institutions of the country, Negro youngsters must get a chance for quality participation.

The fourth point is that you have to restructure the people who run the system, at least formally. That means boards of regents. I gather my neighbor [Kenneth Clark] is the first one of his race who went on the New York State Board of Regents.

Unidentified: The second, but some would say the first.

Eli Ginzberg: That's why I forgot.

Kenneth Clark: The first are the multiple members.

Eli Ginzberg: But in any case, when the faculty of Columbia met with the Trustees for the first meeting after the blow-up, we suggested to the Trustees that it was a little slow of them not to have thought that in New York City, they could have had at least one or two distinguished members of the Negro community among twenty-two members of a board. That might be really good for them. They would have learned something.

Finally, and I think very importantly, the academic institutions, the universities, cannot, at least in the social sciences, be as far from the community environment as they have been. I don't really think you can teach politics or even economics, and surely not government, unless the students have some real relationship to the community in which these problems are real. With the exception of Chicago, I know of no large university in this country that's had anything to do with its environment. That's my fivefold story: curriculum, faculty, student body, organization and control, and community relations.

Black Studies and Black Separatism

Jerome Wiesner: I would like to come back just for a moment to something you talked about at the beginning I think we brushed over too quickly—that's the problem of the teachers colleges. Most of the people who teach in our public schools are coming through the teachers colleges.

Eli Ginzberg: That's not true any more. They come out of liberal arts colleges.

Jerome Wiesner: That's probably because the teachers colleges have changed their names.

Eli Ginzberg: That's right.

Jerome Wiesner: By and large, the quality of the education these people get is very poor. In addition, I think, if you look at where they're coming from in the social structure of this society, this is almost the bottom segment of an upper-middle white population. I think they have deeply ingrained racist problems that have to be dealt with. I think this group needs to talk about that whole problem a little more.

Harold Howe: You all know, I am sure, that there is a major movement abroad now, particularly in elementary and secondary schools, but to some degree in colleges, to offer what is called black history, Negro history. The idea is to present a picture that has been absent to some extent from the curriculum in the schools, particularly in many of the history and social sciences, in some cases to overcompensate, to a degree, by presenting a somewhat romanticized view. There's clearly an effort going forward by textbook manufacturers to realign their texts with this in mind. Regular hearings held on this by Adam Clayton Powell a year and a half ago produced some very interesting evidence to the effect that textbooks had been indeed extremely unfair to minority groups in the United States, either by ignoring them or by making statements about them that were untrue.

C. Vann Woodward: I noticed yesterday that the State of Kentucky, of all places, has passed a bill requiring all students in their public school systems to have Negro history. This movement bears some serious thought and some cautionary remarks. History, as it's used in our educational system and our discourse, reminds me a little bit of the Supreme Court. You remember that the Supreme Court a few years after the Civil War declared segregation to be unconstitutional. About thirty years later *Plessy* v. *Ferguson* declared it to be constitutional, and about a half century later, in the Brown case, the judges changed their mind, and said segregation was unconstitutional. History is used as often to accommodate itself to nationally felt needs and pressure groups. It's under such a demand at present, and as Hal said, it's growing, and I think we'll hear more of it, a good deal more of it. In the program on black studies at Yale, we got the full treatment from the extremists as well as from a few mid-roaders. The extremists told us down the line about the abuse of curriculum and the irrelevance of Virgil and Dante and Shakespeare and Bach and Beethoven and Marcel Proust—that what they really needed was Joe Williams and Duke Ellington and LeRoi Jones and Eldridge Cleaver, that we just weren't with it, and that we also needed black sociology and black economics. I think this movement will continue and perhaps include black biology and black mathematics before it's spent. I think that good came out of this discussion; we learned a great deal that was useful to us.

We have opened up and extended fields of study that were neglected before. We have emphasized more than we had African history, African art, and on the domestic scene problems and concerns that have been unrecognized in any terms in our university curriculum. However, at Yale this is done with our usual faculty supervision. Every course has to be approved by the curriculum committee and every teacher has to be elected to a department at Yale. The black studies is to be under the supervision of departments. I think they will be intelligently handled and answer a great need. But as a cautionary remark about this, this movement is likely to be overdone, misused. I'm afraid the black people are being sold a bill of goods by some of their leaders.

Nationalism is one thing the historians have learned to be especially careful about. It's apparently the most powerful sentiment for most people in the world—not ideology, but nationalism. It's got the Czechs and the Russians at each other's throats. Americans in their early phases of nationalism did really foolish things. In order to establish what they would now call their identity, Americans denigrated everything European in culture and at the same time exalted everything

American. If it was American, it was beautiful, and if it was European, it was not. Of course, that resulted in a lot of third-rate art and letters and sculpture and so forth. I think we have somewhat recovered from our earlier excesses of nationalism in this respect, but by no means are we free from nationalism as a country. The black nationalism, I think, will manifest many of these same excesses. I think this is inevitable, and I think we are going to have to live with it in the colleges, in the public schools, all down the line. We're going to have to adjust to it. I think we must think about it with as much dispassionate wisdom as we can muster, because it's likely to get out of hand.

If it were possible, I would recommend that the federal government subsidize a genial satirist. What some of the phases of this movement need more than anything else is satire. But satire requires humor, and, as you know, this subject has to be discussed with utmost solemnity. That's one of our hangups. That's one reason we're going to be thrown off balance. So I think that one of our recommendations to the government should be some serious planning to include black and white spokesmen to shape the trend of this movement intelligently if possible. The publishers are going to respond to it as the public schools and the government are doing, and they are going to produce some very silly books. Not that that's a new thing. They've produced some awfully silly books before, and many of them have taken the form of racism. But this new movement—we can't blink it, gentlemen—is also racist. It has many of the powerful manifestations of white racism implicit in it. That's one of the ironic things about it. But some of these demands are quite wise; we must, I think, respond to them in a positive way.

Erik Erikson: A satire could be very biting and destructive, if it didn't have a certain amount of insight in it first. Otherwise it could be taken only as a counterattack, and *would* be by the people who feel that, after such a long period of time of submissiveness, they can only gain a certain amount of self-esteem by reasserting . . . I don't think it's exactly nationalism, but it has the personality of a circumscribed group identity which has to use all the methods of propaganda and distortion to show its own values as against other people's.

I was a little disappointed with what you said. You didn't say history has been bad, not just nationalist history. Now, of course, I'm a psychoanalyst, you know that. One can't go around analyzing groups and telling people what is unconsciously behind their racism, but I think there is a level of education young people are ready for today. There are many resistances that do not exist any more. You do not have to break them down. If you speak, for example, of college students going out doing the teaching work, I think the whole college generation would be ready to learn certain insights. I really mean insight—meaning, in a situation where you are up against somebody of another group, to become aware of your own feelings or even to get some inkling of what some of the feelings are that you don't know about, and even meeting with people of the other group.

Now, we can agree that from a religious point of view, from a point of view of law, equality—all men are created equal—is very clear. You can almost enforce it with moralistic stands and say, "You must believe that or else you're bad," or "You are not an American." But what good does it do as long as the people who are as equal as I am don't move into my neighborhood. The moment they become my neighbors, the question, Is he really as equal as I am in this neighborhood or isn't he? comes up. And yet it's not as difficult as it was any more. There's lots of material that can be used from anthropology and social psychology to make the point. I think students could learn that, and I think to some extent they could go out in the community seeing everything we have.

There's not only a generation gap, however, there is a fantastic ideological split as well. People who are convinced, let us say in the anti-Vietnam and pro-Vietnam factions, each develop their own vocabulary, their own standardized, standard explanations. The sides always end up being irreconcilable. I feel the young people have to learn how to speak to another in such a way as to realize why the other can't believe right away what they're saying and also so as to know themselves why *they* can't believe what the other's situation is. But this is very impractical.

Kenneth Clark: I would like to respond to Vann's description of this problem at Yale by adding additional case material from Antioch, Northwestern, and other places where the black students are making demands on colleges and universities. At Antioch, for example, where the protest was made that the existing curriculum was not meeting the needs of the black Antiochians, the black students, who insist on being called "black students," say that they are not getting what they want from college out of books of a white curriculum. The Antioch story is the juxtaposition of black needs and white curriculum in a white college, where one set of courses is suggested for white students, the purpose of which would be to let them understand the nature of the alienation between blacks and whites, and a second group of courses is suggested for black students. I will read this verbatim: "The second set of courses is being given to satisfy the black needs and the black needs only." These courses were said to be open to black students alone.

The Black Studies Institute, which would be the college vehicle within which the black courses could be given, would hire black professionals to teach black students only. Well, as I listened to Vann, I presumed that his calm reflected the academic posture one would assume toward whatever provocations. I am convinced that this represents the major danger to what we are about. If we do not have the courage to face this, to deal with it, we might as well forget any further discussion.

I think it is important to shift this around just a bit and try to understand the problem if it were posed by a group of white students coming to colleges and universities and making these same demands in precisely these same words. I don't think, Vann, that one need hire a satirist for this. I think the movement, itself, is a satire. In fact, these Negro students who say that they are black without regard for their *actual* skin color aren't satirizing American racism. We are confronted with the curious Kafka-like caricature of white racism. To me the fascinating consequence of this is the obscene tolerance, the obscene alacrity and haste, with which the college officials accede to these demands. I am convinced that the felicitousness with which these, to me, thoroughly outrageous, absurd demands are met with a posture of tolerance will have only the consequences of their escalation. What we are seeing—what I think I am seeing—in this charade is that Negro students are really exposing in our colleges and universities the deep ambivalences, racial ambivalences, of the college administrations. They are exposing and exploiting this racial guilt. Also they may be revealing a curious kind of racial cynicism as they watch otherwise seemingly intelligent, a little too sophisticated, and educated persons who are in charge of our colleges acting literally like idiots. Such persons are exposing lack of courage, lack of charity, lack of understanding as to the meaning and function of a university. If Antioch accedes to this, I will resign from their board. The moment they do it I will resign from their board and accuse Antioch of racism.* The colleges and universities acceding to this bizarre caricature of student racism are, in fact, also violating the law. It is a clear violation

* Kenneth Clark resigned from the Board of Trustees of Antioch College on May 16, 1969.

of McLaurin;* it's a clear violation of the civil rights law. And if our group does not have the courage to state this among the other problems of racism and American education as the most significant contemporary example of American racism, then I think we will be in the same position as the colleges and universities. Black racism and white racism are Siamese twins in this regard. It seems to me that acceptance of black racism by white administrations is nothing other than condescension. It is racism in its most subtle, insidious, and basic form, and makes a mockery of education and the goals of education.

Harold Howe: Lisle, did you want to add anything?

Lisle Carter: No, I just came in. I don't know if it's the end or the beginning, but it's a very interesting point. I simply want to observe, and then I think I would like to hear some other comments. It's possible to overstate the case, and I think Ken is overstating it.

Kenneth Clark: Well, I will stand with that overstatement. I don't think, Lisle, that if we were looking at these data in terms of white students' demands of our universities, you would consider other reasonable questions . . .

Lisle Carter: Yes, but that's precisely the point. Reasoning by analogy is certainly one of the weakest forms of reasoning, and you cannot possibly, in the context of this society, seriously compare the whole motivation for demands by black students —whatever you may think of those demands—with similar demands by white students. I think that's such a fallacious analogy, Ken, that it's very hard for me to treat it at a serious level.

* In 1950, the Supreme Court ruled in *McLaurin* v. *Univ. of Oklahoma* that segregating a student from the regular life of the university was harmful to his education.

Kenneth Boulding: How about women students? There is the argument now that women are a lot more different from men than blacks are from whites. And it may well be that we should go back to separate women's colleges. Women are very different and have a very different status, and they are discriminated against much more than blacks are, if I may say so as an economist.

Franklin Roosevelt: Mr. Chairman, I can say that as the former chairman of the Equal Employment Opportunity Commission, which was giving equal rights and opportunities of employment to women as well as to so-called minority groups, I would just like the record to show that I comment unfavorably upon the fact that the only lady present is our hostess.

Christopher Edley: I don't think that Ken has overstated the case in view of a role I see him playing. I personally could never condone racism, whether it is black or white, but the rational process that I go through ends with my having a great deal of tolerance and support for the black student movement. I'll try to give my reasoning.

When black power had its initial thrust, I certainly supported it, and did not feel that I was supporting black racism. I think that the Negro movement through the fifties and sixties reached the point at which it was obvious that Negroes had to disengage and recoup their strength. I think that Negroes proceeded to do this in something of a subconscious manner, and black power was the catch-all word that provided it. The Negro community was saying that through the use of black power, we can use racism as a tool—the only tool readily available for Negroes to identify with each other's developed pride and all of the constructive things that are possible under the rubric of black power.

And we proceeded, I think, to develop a degree of strength. Those who sought to be rational, to develop an ideology in support of this, of course opened a Pandora's box of racism. And perhaps this was part of it all along. I think that now it is clear that some of the excesses of racism are creeping in and that this tool of racism, which we have seen historically used to exploit humanity, is reappearing. I certainly thought during the fifties that the only hope for Negro progress in this country was for Negroes to band together, using black identity as a common thread.

Now some excesses have come to the fore. There is a danger of black nationalism, there is a danger of black separatism that goes beyond the temporary withdrawal to recoup our strength, to regroup and to seek out the powers that we want —the economic and social powers that seem to be attainable for us as a group only through the use of black identity. Now I think that there are roles that Negroes have to play. It seems to me that the power structure has only responded to the excessive demands that have been made in the Negro community, and that there are certain Negroes who because they are bold and courageous, because they have little to lose, must demand things of the power structure which are excessive. And I think that if we—the Ken Clarks and the Chris Edleys and perhaps the Lisle Carters—have a role to play, it is to capitalize on the softening up process that results from the excessive demands.

In conclusion, I would not want the excessive demanders to fail to exploit the power structure—the college presidents, the educators—in demanding everything they can possibly get that would smooth the road for accelerating, for reaching Negro students and giving them the sense of black identification and race pride. This will enable them to band together to overcome the obstacles. I think that subconsciously they are seeking to get into the melting pot and the mainstream of American life. I don't believe that black nationalism will be the major thread. Now, as long as society will only respond to Negro demands when they are made in an excessive fashion, it seems to me that we very much need the courageous students, who unlike their elders, *will sit* at lunch counters, will demand the black-power studies in the colleges.

I don't think that we need condemn them, and I think that many of us get caught in the situation where we have to think as Americans, as Negroes, and perhaps as something in between. And I think that it is possible to identify rationally the roles that people are playing and to realize that really in the long run they complement each other rather than being antagonistic to each other.

Jerome Wiesner: In principle, I can't disagree with you, and I don't think Ken would object to using all the authorities you can muster for integrating lunch counters or to insist on black studies.

Kenneth Clark: I don't know what black studies are, by the way.

Jerome Wiesner: There is something which I think is more destructive, and that is the form of dissent which has induced a certain number of black people in this country to opt out, to say, Well, we wanted a black society of our own somewhere and can't achieve it, obviously. So they spend their time talking about it. And, in a sense, they are not participating in the current effort to do something about the society in which we live.

Clyde Ferguson: I, too, think Ken overstates the case. It's not totally a problem of racism as such. There are elements of it; there is no doubt of that. But I think there is confusion between the rhetoric by which the demands are made and the statements of the demands themselves.

Jerome Wiesner: Do you think a black dormitory is rhetoric?

Clyde Ferguson: No, no.

Kenneth Clark: Or segregated courses in a university are rhetoric?

Donald Ogilvie: I think one reason why there is now a demand for black dormitories is that at most predominantly white institutions not only is there a tacit quota on how many black students come in, but where they go. If you as a black want to room with another black student, you are generally dissuaded from doing so. Your purpose at the university is not just to educate yourself, far from it—your purpose is to be an educational experience for white students. This means that you are disseminated around the university to be part of someone else's learning in their college years. And I can see why other black students, and especially in some of the middle-western schools after being at Wisconsin for a week myself, say all of a sudden, Well the heck with all of this stuff! You know I have something in common with somebody else; we both work in some area; we both have similar interests; I want to room with him. Let's have our own dormitory, to hell with it! Now, if you're going to sit out here and call this "racism," okay. I call it "reasonable reaction" more than anything else. But the fact is that they still want these "excessive" demands, you know, like black studies, like better recruitment, like peace of mind within the context of that white university. Perhaps, consistent with your logic, you might justify the racist tag if they ask for a separate institution altogether, I don't know.

Jerome Wiesner: I think Antioch's claims and demands come pretty close to that.

Franklin Roosevelt: Isn't it a question of exclusivity? The thing that bothers me about the Antioch report that Ken read to us is the exclusivity. I would agree with you, Don: if you want to room with another Negro, that should be your privilege, your right, but I think that if you go as far as to say you want a black dormitory, and you're going to exclude any whites from that dormitory, then I think you're going too far. It's a question of exclusivity.

Donald Ogilvie: As far as I know that wasn't the Northwestern proposal; unfortunately I didn't hear the Antioch one.

Kenneth Clark: "The second set of courses is being given to satisfy the black needs and the black needs only." The leader of this group at Antioch says that these courses are open only to black students.

Franklin Roosevelt: And to be taught only by black professors.

Kenneth Clark: And I contend that it is not an overstatement to charge racism, that it *is* racist on the part of the college or university to accede to any such irrelevant, arbitrary, ignorant demand to attempt to deal with the problems of training human intelligence in terms of the irrelevances of color. And I contend it will be absolutely essential that the NAACP bring suits against any college or university that institutes racially segregated courses or living facilities. If this is not done, it will make a mockery of the years and years of arduous, back-breaking and apparently mind-breaking struggles to remove state-supported institutions as factors in imposing any form of racial segregation on human beings.

And I want to remind you gentlemen who think that I am overstating the case that the legal decisions did not in any way qualify the problem of the irrelevance of race in terms of who initiated the race system. They did not say that the equal-protection clause of the Fourteenth Amendment to the United States Constitution was in some way suspended because blacks voluntarily asked for it. Because these decisions—certainly very clear in McLaurin, and excruciatingly clear in Brown—cannot be abrogated because of the frustrations, the bitterness, the understandable anger of Negro youth or understanding adults, and even more insidiously tolerant liberal whites, who, I repeat, who in obscene taste are willing to accede to this because it does help them to handle their basic racist ambivalence. It does give them a new alibi for racism in America, that Negroes are asking for it.

Eli Ginzberg: I am very sympathetic in general with Ken's approach because I think that we are not making a distinction between group cohesion in itself and group cohesion as a significant instrument of social and human betterment. Obviously, Negroes ought to operate politically with as much cohesion as they can, to change power structures around as much as they can. I'd assume that a university has some standards that are color free as other parts of life are color free. I don't see how it is possible to say, when one looks at phenomena that ought not to be assessed in color terms, that color criteria should be used.

Now I thought, as Ken did, that Vann Woodward was very quiet. I have no doubt that Negroes coming to college have tremendous identity problems. I have no doubt as you said, Mr. Ogilvie, that they get pushed around. It is a white society, and anybody who's in one or another form of a minority, as Kenneth Boulding suggested about women, gets pushed around. Poor people get pushed around; there are white people that come from the back country that get pushed around in this very peculiar society. If you believe that the only answer to being pushed around is to lose all critical discrimination, in the sense that you then have to define an area of blackness for self-protection, you are really going to run great risks.

Let me give you a few illustrations. The military used to run, after all, a segregated world. They did very nice things for the black soldiers. They never held them to account the same way they held white soldiers to account. They used to have separate wards. Anybody who ever ran anything in the military knows that, because they denigrated the black soldiers by putting them in segregated units—because what could you expect from them? They would have less willingness to fight, they would be less clean, they would be more kind. And therefore the trick of running a Negro battalion was always to deal with it as if they were children and animals. Now I am going to argue that it is very dangerous in a competitive world to begin to build up isolated units where general criteria don't apply. I think it is perfectly reasonable to say that Negroes want to have clubs at universities, but this business about Negro courses . . .

Donald Ogilvie: Or black students should even be able to say whom they want for their roommates, right?

Eli Ginzberg: That's correct.

Donald Ogilvie: Like all students.

Eli Ginzberg: But this notion of curriculum affairs. Let me give you the illustration about the Negro and the economics of the ghetto, where I feel I talk with a little bit more understanding of the details. I understand that the Negroes in the ghetto would like to have a piece of the action and so on, but if anybody believes that the economic resolution of Negro discrimination in this country is going to be run successfully by putting things into the ghetto, they're just insane! So that the solution, I think, is to be sure to have tactics appropriate to the phenomena. You can't just throw blackness across the board and assume that therein lies strength.

Clyde Ferguson: I think you can almost do that because of the very pervasiveness of the racism against which the black people are struggling. This is not simply a job of compartmentalizing, because the criterion—that of race—is perfectly clear. You peel back layers and layers of action and, eventually, in every aspect of American society, you run up against the problem of race. One of the difficulties with the whole movement in the fifties, of which I was a part, was the very attempt to say that the problem could be reached at the level of law. That was a delusion. It was wrong. We should have recognized then what we recognize now: that racism is so pervasive that the reaction of group identity is itself going to be pervasive. And there's a great difference between a group which is identified by external pressures applied to it where there is no option, and the group identity which comes by way of an opting into an identifiable situation. It is completely different to deal with the fact that black people decide to band together to do X than it is to deal with the same phenomena where the external pressures banded them together to do X. Completely different. That latter is destruction of humanity. That latter is the fact that he is not a man, that he is unable to make the decisions which every other man in the society makes for himself.

Erik Erikson: I don't think we have a right to call these things immediately by names of the past—colonialism, nationalism, and racism. But that's where I feel the overstatement is, because the overstatement already puts us into categories which are well defined for us and to which we have certain emotional responses and which may not be actually what this is. It's called a "reaction." I must say in this case that the younger member of this group has used a more cautious word than all the older members did, because if you call it a reaction, then you can go and study what kind of a reaction this is. What kind of a transitional phenomenon this is.

Then there is also this problem: Who will deal with it? The administrators have a job of their own, and I certainly feel myself that they should not be pushovers for any of this.

The faculty already has a different job. The faculty has to help, to find, as I pointed out, a certain amount of insight into what kind of a transitional phenomenon this is. If you want to discuss it in terms of identity, that would be a much more difficult thing than the loose use of this word would imply, because real identity is the thing that comes out of history, economics, daily lives, and so on. You don't just get it by saying, "I am such and such and I feel I'm all right." Identity is a very complex social and psychological phenomenon. You would have to expect that there would be very, very difficult transitional phenomena, each of which have had to be dealt with as they come up. Now, again, what's left out is what are the other students going to do about it? And I predict a white sit-in in a Negro dormitory. Some white students would say: we are not going to be excluded from this.

Harold Howe: Like Northwestern . . .

Erik Erikson: Somebody has to show that you cannot meet it with moralistic, old-fashioned terms, and you cannot slap it down. You have to deal with it—I don't know how. I would think in terms of, almost in civil rights terms now, that the message has been taken over by people who now are going to be discriminated against by black nationalists.

Thomas Pettigrew: I want to go back down the road just a bit on the other side of Ken's formula, that is, the whites' response, the ready and prompt white response in Northwestern. The fact is, in the second round of demands, not in the first round, the black students' group offered two alternatives to Northwestern which were not widely publicized in the press. One alternative, favored by the leading group but not favored by the majority, was followed—the Black Student Union demand. But the other demand was, instead, to end exclusive racist all-white fraternities at Northwestern. What, I must say, seared my soul about the Northwestern action was the readiness with which the Northwestern administration chose to escalate injustice without even seriously considering abolishing the exclusive white fraternities.

Now, that would lead me to believe that there are two things to remember. One, I like Don's word "reaction," and this is—among some students and not among all—this is the feeling of despair and desperation. I think much of the derogation these days of integration is not of integration at all but of desegregation that didn't make it. It seems that's what you're describing, Don, when you describe the situation in which the Negro students are essentially used for the purposes of the administration. A kind of mechanical form of desegregation. It is this alienation from the desegregated situation that I believe is at the core of it, and I don't think that the reaction, or whatever you want to call it, is likely to change. It will change its form, but I don't think the feeling and the push will change until what it is reacting to changes.

I think administrators can help. I agree with you, Erik— they can't do it all. I think the Northwestern administrators could have helped by taking the right alternative when it was offered to them by the students. But until the fact that there is something like integration, cross-racial acceptance, we will have one kind of a response or another.

I would like to add one more footnote. A disturbing personal thing at Harvard, it seems to me, is that now the movement is at such a level there—and on some other campuses —that there is a tyranny among the black students themselves. Some feel very strongly the way we are describing the whole group, some do not. Those who do not are under great pressure to sit at, eat at, tables where there are otherwise all white students. They come under pressure for weeks, and they report this and that tyranny individually to me. I don't think we should overgeneralize that all black students feel exactly the same way.

Donald Ogilvie: I withdraw my word "reaction," because it's been used, misused, and obscenely abused. Despair and desperation is what people have tacked on to reaction. All right, all I will try to say is what black students have done is to assert themselves. In the Northwestern situation, I don't agree that the proper reaction of the administration would have been *just* to desegregate or open up white fraternities. The proposal put to the administration was that if whites were indeed conscious of social justice, they should provide, you can call it a black dormitory, but a dormitory ostensibly for those black students who wanted to room together and could room there. Any white students who wished to room in that dorm could opt in. That was always open. You've been talking about the injustice of an exclusive all-black dormitory—nowhere has there been a request for an exclusive all-black dormitory with no whites allowed. To date that request has been made nowhere. There has been the Antioch request for studies just for black students. That's one place, and I don't believe all the ramifications of that request have been discussed or appreciated. Also there have been demands put to several other administrations, not just this one. So why pick out Antioch? Perhaps that is your desperation and despair. Perhaps they were "reacting." I can't comment further on this except to say most students have recognized, identified phenomena and decided they were going to act on it in the direction they thought was best.

Now to another point. It disturbs me when you talk about those black students at Harvard who feel they're under pressure, that they're beset for weeks. Generally, even those I know up there say that isn't the case for most. These fellows might feel hung up because they're undergoing their own ID thing, because they see some black students going a totally different way from the direction they're going. The others are not trying to make it; they're not trying to be a part of the totally integrated setting at all times; and they're not trying to work their way into the white world proper. They're not that interested in the "mainstream." So I don't think these fellows who have their own individual hangups are a proper province for this conference to deal with. And I think that, again, you are adding to this overstatement, trying to sensationalize by even bringing it up.

Thomas Pettigrew: My own point is that there are differences, that's all.

Donald Ogilvie: There are differences. There are not all white people as members at this table. This, as your point, is almost academic.

Harold Howe: We got into this discussion on the basis of various concepts of materials that are used and not used in schools and colleges and those that may be created in the future. It does occur to me that there are very few secondary schools in the United States where this kind of a discussion could have taken place. The resources among the teachers in those schools are inadequate to sustain such discussion. They'd be threatened by it; yet it is terribly important that such a discussion as we are having around the table here somehow be made possible in the context of at least the secondary school and the college. And in the lower levels, whatever leads to elementary exposure to the fact that race is something in the world that people have feelings about and that this is a reality that children in their lives are going to have to contend with increasingly. It's something the schools need to adjust to in some fashion or other. And I suspect that the practical methods of reaching in this direction first of all have to do with major changes in teacher training and that such discussions as this need very much to be a part—much more in the United States—of teacher training activities. I know literally hundreds of teacher training institutions that would shy away from any effort to create such an exposure and the problems that go with it. There is one area that needs to rethink its activities—the teacher training area—in terms of preparing people to have enough exposure to the problem to be some resource to their students later on.

Black Colleges and White Colleges

Milton Galamison: There are two things in our preliminary statement that I would like to see modified, in case we never get back to it. Suggesting that black colleges be closed is the kind of thing which must make Mr. Ogilvie bristle. It shouldn't be that we just close black colleges, but that we would seek to integrate all colleges.

Kenneth Clark: Close the white ones, too.

Milton Galamison: There should be a balancing out. If we maintain black colleges, we integrate them, if we maintain white colleges, we integrate them.

The second thing that bothers me is the statement, "the compensatory and enrichment programs could obscure the basic issue of impossibility of high quality education for all children in segregated schools." I would be inclined to think that this is true, but I would hesitate ever to put it in writing, because I don't think any segregated school has really had an opportunity. Well, we did—we had twenty-six in Brooklyn, underwritten by the Ford Foundation, which several years ago did achieve high academic standards, but I would rather say on an issue like this that, in terms of education in the finest sense of the term, we should not settle for all-segregated black schools or racially apartheid schools, black or white. I would rather put it in that context than to make a bold statement like "there can be no high-quality education at an all-black school."

Eugene Patterson: Mr. Chairman, are we for integration or aren't we? Are the Supreme Court, the Coleman report,* the Civil Rights Commission,† and all the major studies done in the field all wrong in saying that segregated education is inherently inferior? If they're wrong, I think we could make a headline by saying so, but if they're right, I don't think it's at all ceremonial to restate this, and in light of the tremendous changes that Mr. Ogilvie represents, I think that we ought to discuss this matter. Are we still for integration as the long-range goal of American society?

Harold Howe: What we say in this document is that integration should be on the agenda as both a short- and a long-range goal, and we then go on to observe that in some places it's possible now, in other places more difficult now and will necessarily be a longer-range goal.

Eugene Patterson: I recognize this, but Mr. Galamison has taken some exception to this particular point. And my only fear is that if we begin to erode the principle, if we begin to waver and say, well, maybe segregated education *is* all right, those masses who want segregation are going to demand it.

Thomas Pettigrew: I agree with Reverend Galamison that the statement is poorly put. I think it should state that many people fear that if you say the first priority is integration, you are saying you would then ignore the schools as they now exist in the ghetto. I've been quoted as saying that in terms I don't believe I've ever used. I think it is better to say that, even with integration as first priority, you do everything in ghetto schools you're doing in others, provided that what you're doing is not

* James S. Coleman, *et al., Equality of Educational Opportunity* (Washington, D.C., U.S. Government Printing Office, 1966).

† Otto Kerner, *et al., Report of the National Advisory Commission on Civil Disorders* (New York, E. P. Dutton, Inc., 1968).

counterproductive for integration. It should be the rule of the test you make of enrichment programs. I think many of our enrichment programs have, in fact, not been enrichment at at all but devices for preventing integration. Once you exclude that classification, enrichment programs, you can without hesitation favor them.

Christopher Edley: Mr. Chairman, picking up on that and going back to the Negro colleges, I'd like to state my own personal position: that the statement on closing Negro colleges, even if you try to strike a balance, is a very dangerous one and will have to be very carefully thought out. I am reminded of the specific case involving Negro law schools, predominantly Negro law schools in the South, where a few years ago an accreditation committee of the American Bar Association came out in a very liberal voice saying that those schools should be closed down, that Negro lawyers should be trained in an integrated setting. It was a great statement by liberals. This resulted in several Southern states taking steps to close their Negro law schools. The accreditation committee has now, several years later, reversed itself and has made a special plea that additional resources be pushed into these schools because they're needed during an interim period. It may be that in fifteen or twenty years we can do away with them. The same thing is true of Negro colleges. We don't begin to have the educational resources to discard them. In making a fine liberal statement, we may be giving ammunition to those who will act, following through on this by closing those schools in the next few years, further shortening the amount of resources available. It's a very difficult problem. You have to spell out the dimensions. You're not talking about doing away with Negro colleges within the next four or five years. If it is something of a long-range and desirable goal, it should be stated that way, but in terms of the dangers that I am trying to spell out.

C. Vann Woodward: Just a footnote to that. The severest critics of the Negro colleges in the South, Dave Riesman and Christopher Jencks—whether you agree with them or not— with all their criticism have underlined what has been said, I think, by saying they simply are indispensable for a long time to come, and it would be a mistake to take an unrealistic stand about them.*

Clyde Ferguson: I have a more fundamental objection to closing Negro colleges, and it's not simply a question of present resources. There's an enormous diversity in colleges and ought to be an enormous diversity in the missions that particular colleges have. I certainly distinguish between the college which is required to be segregated by law, which is wholly objectionable, and the college which is not required to be racially separate, but through its own resources, out of its own community, through its own mission, has staked out for itself a particular role. The criticism of the Negro colleges may be that they have, in too many instances, been pallid, unresourceful imitations of the white colleges. But there is a role and there *is* a mission, at this time in our society and for a long time to come, for this kind of a college, which has as its center the problem of the education, the transitional education that will go on for another two or three generations of a group that has been excluded in the past. Consequently I object to the notion of phasing out or doing away with Negro colleges; I'd much rather see a statement which would remind the existing institutions that they have a special mission relating to a particular group, and, if they're not responsive to that particular mission, that then they have no justification for being, that it's not just simply another skin game or another appropriate racial mix.

Eli Ginzberg: Do you mean that you would not want to have any white faculty members there?

* Christopher Jencks and David Riesman, *The Academic Revolution* (New York, Doubleday, 1968).

Clyde Ferguson: No, not at all, not at all. . . .

Eli Ginzberg: Does it mean that you would not allow a minority of white youngsters who happen to be in the neighborhood who would like to attend?

Clyde Ferguson: *Not at all.* Not at all. As a matter of fact, if you were defining the mission of this college, it is a mission which relates itself to the underprivileged, the uneducated class that has not been able to get out of the system what the middle and upper classes get out of it. With that particular mission you're going to deal with a lot of people who are not Negro, but who have problems of the same character. The college has a special mission, and we ought to recognize that not every college is going to be performing the same mission that Harvard or Yale or Columbia performs in the society. There are other missions for colleges, and to be a pale, artificial imitation is to be a wasteful resource.

C. Vann Woodward: Careful! What about the well-known mission of the University of Alabama?

Clyde Ferguson: Some missions are unacceptable.

Jerome Wiesner: There are some colleges that are less inadequate than others. The reason there are inadequate ones is that, catering as they do to this poor segment of the society, they don't get any resources. They've been doing a little better than they have in the past. It seems to me if we do conclude that this is an important element, as we seem to be coming around to, we ought also to say something about trying to support them.

Clyde Ferguson: Precisely. It's the first point related by Eli Ginzberg yesterday: that, in fact, allocation of resources in the educational process has followed a racial line, and these colleges reflect it.

Jerome Wiesner: You see it no more clearly than you do in the colleges in the South.

Milton Galamison: May I say this, which may not be kind, but I want to say it: that inherent in a statement like this is a kind of racial arrogance. You're saying, We got problems with segregated colleges—let's close down all the black colleges. What does this mean to black people? They are going to have token representation on boards of some white colleges. It would have to be done on the assumption that all white colleges will now have fair admission policies, but this is not true. Many black people need these colleges because they can get into them when they can't get into the white colleges. And my whole point is to balance the thing out. The whole situation is so distorted that anything you say almost sounds wrong or questionable. All I'm saying is that we say we're going to try to do away with all segregated institutions by integrating. If you want to integrate the white ones, then let's integrate the black ones. It seems to me we would be on sounder ground, taking a position like this than saying, Let's shut down black colleges. The point is, the more we move toward some kind of just situation, the more we make these other distorted situations unnecessary.

Somebody said a while ago, you know, you can't bring much moral solution to some of our problems, but I think we can. I think the more we deal morally—I don't mean in terms of preaching or anything like that—with some of these problems, the more we make these grotesque things unnecessary. If you really had a fair situation, you'd put segregated colleges out of business over a period of time.

Franklin Roosevelt: Milton, I agree with everything you said, but would you add to that that additional resources somehow must be made available to the black colleges so the levels of achievement of standards and, therefore, their attractiveness to blacks can be raised for the benefit of the whole community of which they are a part.

Milton Galamison: I would go along with that.

Kenneth Clark: I wanted to put in this statement, and I kept it in, in spite of pressures raised by wiser heads at 1:00 A.M. this morning—and precisely for the reasons that you've just stated: that Negro and white colleges are an anachronism.

I would agree completely with you that Negro colleges and white colleges be eliminated, because the policy of education by race is inimical to education. But, in addition, there is the reality that the existence of Negro colleges is a manifestation of, a contribution to, the institution of racism. You have a concrete example of elimination of the Negro college precisely in the direction that you suggest—West Virginia State. That was eliminated as a Negro college and became—a college. You also have the problem of inadequate facilities. And a third problem would be—to get right at the heart of racism—double standards. Double standards of accreditation. Double standards of meanings of degrees. Double standards of content. Invariably these double standards are in the direction of inferior standards for the Negro college, which again makes the college an institutionalized racist phenomenon. So when we say the elimination of Negro colleges, we mean the elimination of all of these contextual things which support and reinforce racism so that a Negro kid comes out of a college with obviously inadequate resources. He allegedly has an A.B.—which is not an A.B. in terms of competitive function. If we do not address ourselves to the elimination of this, then we are not addressing ourselves to a very important part of racism in American education.

Eli Ginzberg: Well, I think it might help to build a bridge. I think that what Ken said is right, but there is a remaining problem that ought to be noted. That is, after all, we've had a nonracist public education, higher educational institution in New York for a long time—Ken teaches there. It's very hard to find Negroes there in any large numbers. . . .

Kenneth Clark: That's because of the quality of their secondary and elementary education.

Eli Ginzberg: That's right. Now, since the secondary and the elementary education is not going to really give substantial equality for a long time, because you just can't turn it around that fast, you at least have to say that public funds must be apportioned to members of minority groups and opportunities made available for them in some kind of an appropriate fashion. When the Navy became desegregated, they turned right around and used educational standards, so the second time around it wasn't a Negro that you left out, you just left them out on the basis of education. The Army and the Air Force didn't want to play that game, and they managed to have some Negroes. You have to be very careful therefore, especially given the Southern states and American institutions for what they are, to make sure that the flow of funds is related to the needs of the minorities. Otherwise you're going to be in trouble. Otherwise you'll have desegregated city colleges as we have in New York, and no Negroes will go.

INTEGRATION AS END AND AS MEANS

James Allen: Well, I'd like to come back a little bit to Mr. Patterson's earlier question and make this statement: I think we are for integration and very strongly for integration, but I think we've got to place first the very best education that can be devised here and now for every individual, wherever he is. You don't let the goal of segregation stand in the way, or the goal of integration stand in the way of trying to do the very best you can for those where they are now.

The reason I'm so concerned about the structural aspect is that it's not just the integration problem or the Negro youngster that has been suffering from the barriers of traditional patterns of organizing and financing the schools—it's all youngsters. The small high school makes it impossible to provide good education for anybody who happens to be there. But I would emphasize that I don't think segregation and the goal of integration and the efforts to provide good—call it compensatory or what, but good—education for everyone wherever he is now are opposite goals at all.

Eugene Patterson: I'm for compensatory education to meet the practical problem now.

James Allen: So am I.

Eugene Patterson: I'm for integration as a national goal. But I have the feeling that in this debate, and I think it is rather important, no priority has really been set, and I think that this meeting, if it is an action meeting, ought to set a priority, because the Commissioner of Education can't go to Congress with a program unless he knows what the national goal is going to be. Is he just going to tinker around with the ghetto school where it is, or is he going to have a national goal so that he can go to Congress and ask for experimental money to try an educational park in selected cities? Do we recommend this? Is it a good idea? And going back to your idea for some structural changes, should we recommend that local financing of schools be discontinued in this country?

Harry Rowen: I would argue the following propositions: that the only thing that is really going to make a significant difference, to white attitudes, to racism in the United States on the white side, is the perception of Negro achievement. Short of achievement there really won't be fundamental change. Achievement in lots of dimensions. If it turns out, say, a hundred years from now that a Negro kid getting out of grade school in New York is three grade levels behind in reading skills, white attitudes are not going to be very different a hundred years from now than from what they are today. I think that fact dominates and overrides a lot of other things.

Now, if one accepts that, then one might take as an objective—more important than a lot of other objectives with respect at least to the racism issue—an objective like equal achievement. Equal achievement. Not just equal opportunity, but equal results, equal performance, and equal achievement. Then look at the programs and ask, Does this program look as though it's got a chance? Has it real promise for producing that objective: equal achievement? Centralize financing, decentralize city school systems, put more money in, have Negro separatism—look at the instruments from the point of view of whether they will produce that result, or maybe if modified will produce that result. It seems to me that to the extent we really are concerned about racism, we'd really have to accept something like this objective. Equal performance for the system—and then design programs to fit it.

Unidentified: Does this disavow desegregation or integration?

Harry Rowen: It doesn't disavow it.

Unidentified: Is it secondary?

Harry Rowen: I would think that it should be regarded as secondary on the grounds that it isn't going to work without something like equal achievement. By the way, if integration can be plausibly and persuasively argued as an instrument for equalizing performance . . .

Kenneth Clark: This goes back to Jim's point, that this is precisely what we argue on different grounds.

Harry Rowen: Many of the same instruments might be used, but not necessarily.

Clyde Ferguson: There's a fundamental difference of treatment. If integration or segregation is treated as a tactical tool to reach the problem of equality of achievement, that is quite different from integration as a goal, which says if you get the right skin color then you have reached that goal. Because the same bad dissimilar performances can take place in *that* context as can take place in a separate context. Consequently, I think the real vice is the way in which we have said "integration." It means to a lot of people what it shouldn't mean. It does mean to a great many of the public: get the right schoolmates. Get buses and get the skins mixed, and then that problem is solved. Integration is the tool we are actually using to combat the racist phenomenon that when something became all black, it became short-changed. Consequently society won't operate in any other way, unless you mix up the people so that this particular mechanism in the society can no longer work. Then when you get to the point where the society can no longer use race as a criteria for allocating resources, integration will have performed its goal. Then you deal with, I think, what we are really after—and that is the quality of education. The reason why the legal cases were brought was the fact that society consistently short-changed the separate institution.

Kenneth Clark: I'd like to point out to Clyde, perhaps presumptuously because he's a lawyer and I'm not, that this is precisely the reasoning stated in the Brown decision, in practically those words.

Clyde Ferguson: It's been a misconception that once you reach the goal of that proper skin mix, you are through with the problem. You may be through with it if the resources begin to be reallocated without regard to race. But to a certain extent, I think that is a straw man.

James Allen: It's really the quality that you're after.

Clyde Ferguson: Quality in what, though?

Milton Galamison: You know, it may be true that we will find more acceptance as black people if we achieve certain standards, but it's almost as difficult, in the present structure, as trying to be *white* in order to be accepted, because it's almost impossible in this structure for our kids to achieve the kind of comparable standards that we would all like to see. We are the victims, and I use that word advisedly, of the same standards and tests and Regents' exams, and the whole business, as white children are in the culture, but we are not the beneficiaries, and I use *that* word advisedly, of the same attitudes. So we can endlessly be put through these kinds of tests under the present structure and always come up short—looking like a race of idiots and then being condemned and isolated and segregated on the basis of a performance which was almost impossible in terms of expectations in the first place.

When Dr. Ginzberg outlined what he thought were five problems, I think this somehow speaks to the whole issue. I was trying to measure the whole decentralization concept alongside those five problems to see how decentralization for black people brings some resolution to these problems, and I'd like to take just a minute or two to talk about it.

But first, I'd like to say what my own feeling is about integration. I don't think we can *ever* have education in the deepest, finest sense of the term for black people or white people in an apartheid school system. We just can't. But I want to add, too, that in many instances I find we are not talking about education at all; we're talking about vocational training; we're talking about preparing people to pass tests; we're talking about preparing people to make more money; and we're not really talking about education. Nobody really thinking about education, black or white, could be talking about a separatist school system, because, apart from these other things that we've been discussing is the whole picture, is the whole—and, Ken, you can do this much better—psychological, the whole philosophical attitude towards life which you're developing within the framework of the school situation —the learning situation.

You know, the word that I've been hearing all around for two days, and nobody has really said it, is ethnocentrism. Basically, I think, this is what we're talking about. When one gentleman talks about black teachers who aren't meeting standards, either, because there is a cultural differential between black-educated teachers and the black children they're teaching and whites, we're talking about ethnocentrism. When we're talking about the white teacher coming up short because of her attitudes or the whole structure as being indifferent to the black people, we're talking about ethnocentrism. And somehow this is a kinder word to use, in some instances, than racism, which people deny.

But to your five points, Dr. Ginzberg: You talk about the allocation of funds. In a decentralized system what the black community is saying is, Let us have our own funds. We want a per capita quota like everybody else, we want the same capital construction funds like everybody else, but let us handle our own funds. Now there is some illusion at work here, in the sense that people see themselves spending money when they really will only be handling vouchers, but this has to be learned. Still there is this concept that whoever holds the purse calls the tune, and the black community is saying let us handle the purse strings to the degree that it is feasible—and on as equal a basis as anybody else.

Your second point was that education leadership is not committed to educating poor groups and race groups. Well, in a decentralized system, the educational leadership becomes transferred to the community, whatever the community may be, if it's poor people, if it's black people. And because it is transferred to the community, the community becomes the educational leadership, and this differential, this gap is bridged, you know, between whatever differences may exist between those who are bringing the teaching and those who hope to benefit from the learning. The black community thinks in terms of accountability—that the teaching structure in New York City, for example, has never been really accountable to the community. This is why people have to picket to get rid of a teacher, or picket to get rid of a principal, because they're not really accountable. They're accountable downtown, where the misunderstanding may be even greater than it is between the teacher, who's there, and the community. Decentralization would hope to overcome this kind of a problem.

The curriculum was the third point. It is not constructive, not designed to meet the needs of poor groups and racial groups. Well, inherent in this whole process of decentralization is community participation in the development and cultivation of the curriculum with expert advice and help—consultant help, of course.

The next point you set out was on remedial action of malperformance of the system, and here again we come back to the accountability thing, where, in New York City, for example, you have a school system which is fed mostly by an archaic Board of Examiners that ought to be abolished, which in seventy years of its existence has never determined whether its method of choosing teachers gets the best teachers or not, and you have on the other hand a union which makes it almost impossible to have a teacher fired, so that you have only about twelve teachers who have been fired in the last five years—regular teachers—and the community system suffers. So if we are talking about malperformance, if the malperformance is in the structure to even a greater degree than it is in the local school, you keep on with this remedial business when the real reform ought to be in the whole structure. If we had decentralization, we could resolve this problem, because some system would be developed to evaluate teachers and principals on an objective basis. They could not be defended in their malfunctioning if the students were not producing and the teachers were not producing.

The final point is, of course, the one we have been arguing all the time, that we must decide for integration, and I think we have decided *for*, I think everybody you know would conceive that unity is better than disunity, that togetherness is better than apartness. But on the other hand, we are faced with all of these other real practical problems in the black community, and in many white communities which make integration a goal. It seems to me it's a matter of emphasis at this point whether we are going to emphasize one goal or the other. But, certainly, I think it is the objective for everybody to have a system in which segregation for white or black kids is a thing of the past.

Lisle Carter: We're trying to affect racism in the society, we're trying to affect racism in the school system, and we're trying to provide quality education; we're trying to bring about institutional change, and we're sort of mixing these all up back and forth. Obviously they overlap, but we don't define in any sensible way *how* they overlap. I think that what you find here, as probably in every other institutional area of American life, is that the institutional hardening and complexity make much more difficult the problem of dealing with race because they have developed during our extremely racistic period when we altogether ignored what was happening to Negroes in this country. That being the case, it seems to me that what you end up saying is that you cannot solve some of these problems dealing with race without solving some of the basic institutional problems that involve education.

You might say the same thing of public welfare, or whatever area you get into, and yet it does not come through in this document. Now what Harry is obviously referring to, and I think it is salutary, is that the educational people won't stand for any output measures on what they do. We keep talking about quality of education as if that's a good in itself without any goals about what it is you're trying to accomplish in the educational system itself. Now the fact that we're hung up on is that we are painfully conscious that there are millions of kids now in the school system today who will not benefit from our deliberations unless we can find some way to balance the considerations of where we're trying to go in the society with what we're trying to do for youngsters in the school system. And it seems to me that we ought to recognize the terrible problem of getting institutional change and how difficult it will be in the school system and some of the ways in which that needs to be accomplished.

For example, we talk about decentralization of the schools in administration. I'm surprised to find it under improving the quality of education rather than bringing about instituttional change. I can see you can make an argument for both, but it seems to me that it is put here in its worst possible context. We could say an alternative to decentralizing large schools is employing parents as teacher aides and so on. You know, this is rather trivial in the context of what you're trying to accomplish, it seems to me. We could clarify this by stating specific goals.

SELF-IMAGE AND ACHIEVEMENT

Harold Howe: I think that is very helpful, Lisle. Let me make an observation, if I may, on both your and Harry's points about outward measurement, because I think that it was primarily stated in terms of achievement as far as Harry was concerned, and I think you're quite right that educational organizations and groups are generally opposed to this sort of thing—violently opposed—so that, in terms of political relationships, it is an extremely difficult sort of thing to move on. That doesn't mean that it shouldn't be moved on, but I think there are people outside of educational organizations and groups who are threatened by this, and therefore do object, who have some concern about using achievement measures for the purpose of either avoiding teachers or even judging the excellence of school programs. Some persons are concerned first of all about the adequacy of these measures, who see that it is quite possible to develop an IQ test for youngsters from the Kentucky mountains on which they will show a high IQ and on which sophisticated youngsters from the suburbs will show a low IQ, and to administer to these same two groups of youngsters another set which will reverse the IQs. I think this kind of concern gets into the minds of people who realize that our achievement measures, and our measures of capacity for achievement, are in an early state of development. We need a good deal more sophistication before we make the whole system depend on these things.

Harry Rowen: The system is already dependent on these things.

Harold Howe: The system makes some use of these things. Many people are inclined to think overuse. Now, another area which has to do with the purpose of education and some of the other values of education besides achievement—Jim Coleman, if I recall correctly, in his report addressed himself at some length to this problem—is how a person feels about himself and his own self-image, as the phrase goes. And the importance of that to him as an individual and indeed the importance of that to his ultimate success.

Kenneth Clark: If he can't read?

Harold Howe: No, I'm not denying, Ken, this is a factor, but I'm saying there's another whole series of values here that aren't measured in terms of achievement tests, which are in themselves to some degree invalid. . . . There is a third point that I was trying to talk to yesterday and not doing very well —the very great difficulty of using achievement tests realistically for administrative purposes, where there is real payoff placed on them, when you know something about the very wide range of human differences and the fact that it is unreasonable to expect some white children, some Mexican-American children, some black children, to reach beyond certain levels of capacity of generalization, certain levels of capacity of performance in school in the achievement sense. This isn't a matter that goes with race—there is a human differential that does exist in all schools.

Lisle Carter: But Harold, what do we say about that school in Washington that you know about where not a single youngster in the whole school could read at the national average? What do you say about that?

James Allen: It's 48 percent in New York City.

Harold Howe: I say that *that* school needs a total revolution. I'd like to see this sort of thing tried experimentally, but I have many doubts about the workableness of a revolution which says to that faculty, You're a totally inadequate group because you didn't make these kids read. I'm somewhat more hopeful about the kind of approach that says to that faculty, Clearly there's a problem here; you've got to work on it with us—you're the people who are going to have to be in that school—there are going to be a lot more people like you in the years ahead, and we need to find a way to train you, we need to get new kinds of materials in that school, we need to pay attention to the output these produce. But to enter into a system of blame on the individual teacher in any way, without a lot more knowledge of that sort of thing than I think we have, and into a kind of accountability that is suggested in this document at this point worries me.

Christopher Edley: Hal, I think we are all tied up with that, but what disturbs me in what you say is that education as it is played now is a game. I played this game. I'm a winner in the game to a certain extent. You're talking about changing some of the values and objectives of people who are caught up in that game, but you aren't changing the rules of the game. You're saying that it's O.K. for society to judge them, it's O.K. for them to fail college admission tests, it's O.K. for them to return on the basis of the rules as they exist now. You know it's a luxury talking about the fifth-grader who is not achieving now, talking in terms of there being some higher esoteric values in education and how it doesn't matter whether he could qualify for college or get into the vocational trade that he wants to get into. But, as I see it, that kid must achieve by the rules. If you talk about changing the admission rules for colleges first, or the job qualifications, or the credentials that the boss requires, and then you go back and change the course of education for that kid in the system, then I'm a thousand percent with you. But if you talk about changing his education, the nature of his education, before you start changing the rules that he's going to run into in life, then I'm deeply disturbed. I'd hate for this kid to have to fight a ruthless, cutthroat, competitive game in education, but I don't know any alternative—if we are to give him a fair break in making it in life as we know it today.

Kenneth Clark: I would like to support Chris on this, and to add a footnote that if a youngster does not have a realistic basis in achievement for his self-esteem, he inevitably will be thrown back on paranoia for self-esteem. If you have double standards, double rules, you know these are schools that are consistently underachieving. Within those schools you have teachers who, the record shows, consistently contribute to retardation—though, fortunately, some teachers who consistently try and succeed in compensating for some of the retardation they inherit. And if you try to obscure this by saying, Well, there are some other things which these kids are getting such as feeling good about themselves— I don't know a single Negro kid who feels good about himself retarded. He's mad as hell. He's mad at the school; he's mad at the teachers; he's mad at society; he's mad at whitey and he's mad at blacky. Most of them have to resort to compensatory paranoia for their inadequate achievement, which they are more painfully aware of than these educators, who are trying to tell him that he feels good about himself five years retarded in reading.

Harold Howe: Well, don't read into this, Ken, that I'm trying to advocate simply everybody feeling good and not learning anything. . . .

Kenneth Clark: Nobody can feel good not learning anything.

Harold Howe: There is really no intention of that on my part. I think that there are some very subtle relationships, however . . .

Kenneth Clark: Aren't there good teachers and bad teachers?

Harold Howe: Oh, sure. But I think that also— Take integration. It seems to me that it's a means as well as an end. People talk about that here. It is possible that pressure on integration will help to produce the sense of belonging to and having a chance in the larger society, which will in turn help to produce achievement.

Kenneth Clark: But Chris's point was really the role of education in providing individuals with opportunities for competition, having the skills to compete, rather than being handicapped. And I suppose one reason we jumped on this "feeling good" is because it is just the kind of thing that we have been fed. You can feel good as an exotic primitive who is an absolutely unsalable commodity because there aren't but so many tap dancers and but so many football players that society can absorb. The rest of us have to really get out there and compete and compete with equipment and skills provided by education.

Harold Howe: Just let me make one further observation, Eli: that whites aren't just competing on achievement, they're competing on their racial superiority.

Kenneth Clark: But they're basically using the educational system to reinforce that and to handicap lower-status people.

Harold Howe: And, therefore, it seems to me, there is a significant matter in getting the education system arranged so that it does not in any fashion reflect racial inferiority for a particular group. I think that segregation does reach in that direction, so there is both an achievement goal and other related goals connected with integration.

RACISM AND ALLOCATIONS

Eli Ginzberg: I have a suggestion for you, since this is, after all, a conference on racism and education. I think you ought to list and get an agreement on ten major aspects where racism is operative in education. And I would say one thing that I have said before—racism gives you too little resources for minorities. It gives you the worst kind of teacher, because the teachers are badly prepared, and you get the youngest teachers, circulating teachers, and so on. You get the worst facilities, by and large. You get lousy guidance, one of the most racist aspects of this whole damn affair, when you tell Negro kids that they can't "go anywhere," etc.

So, I would list ten points and stop. Then I would say what

one is interested in doing. I would attempt to get agreement from this group to say we're interested in trying to reduce as rapidly as possible these injurious, insidious, unjust aspects of racism, moving toward a concept immediately—you can't really say it—of an integrated society, which of course involves integrated schools. But that, you know, is a long-term operation. That can't be done so easily without housing and a lot of other things. Then I think you want to list under three headings how you make progress within this goal, moving towards an integrated society, with integrated schools. You want to indicate what you want to do on the resource front—which is financing and manpower—what you want to do on the administration and structure front to get rid of these things, and what you want to do on teachers and curriculum. You must call attention to what racism is. It's an evil that runs all the way through this thing.

Elinor Gordon: Before we adjourn, giving us enough time to discuss, I'd love to know from this group whether they have any idea that this country is ever going to move in these directions; whether it will ever be a national policy that we educate our children for equality, and whether there is going to be such a will in this country, whether it can be developed. Is this a question that we don't dare ask?

Franklin Roosevelt: Let me say, that I am, perhaps by nature, an optimist. I am thinking now of something perhaps comparable. We have seen in the last twenty-five or maybe thirty years a development within the business community of a new sense of its obligations and responsibilities to the nation and to the communities in which it operates. And if we go back to the first quarter of this century, we see a business leadership attitude completely 180 degrees opposite. The only purpose of business leadership was to make money, to dominate its community. Those of us who remember the coalfields in West

Virginia and Kentucky, the company store, the company housing realize how far and vast a change of business attitude has
come about in the last twenty-five years. And so I use that as
a basis for my optimism that this country is changing, that it
is becoming responsible in its attitudes towards the role of education and to the fundamental policies that we have been
talking about here. So I, Elinor, am an optimist, and I think
I am an optimist with good reason.

Elinor Gordon: Well, Franklin, excuse me, I'm sorry. I'd just
like to say that Reverend Galamison and Commissioner Allen
and we of New York are bloodied and a bit bowed—we've
been coping with the educational structure in New York City.
And we haven't talked about how and what you do to the
structure, really, after you get the set of things you'd like to
do to them.

Clyde Ferguson: Madame Chairman, I think if I could put
one footnote on that: there is a will, in all these people born
after 1945 sitting in administration buildings and disrupting
the system. The will is there and the recognition is there and,
in one sense, our problem is not to stand too much in the way
of the changes which they are forcing on the system. The
only problem with it is that they have recognized the same
thing that we recognized around the table about the difficulty
of structural change. But they come up with the conclusion
that it is about time to stop writing reports and making statements, that the only way you get the system to respond to their
will, which I think is the right will, is to stop the system and
disrupt it with meat axes or sit-ins, peaceful or otherwise. The
real tactical problem is whether or not that will can be chan-
neled in a way that's still credible to the students of that
generation of people born after 1945, showing them that in
fact the structure *is* responding, rather than behaving like the
balloon we have seen in the past. It responds and then when
the fist is taken out the balloon comes back.

Harold Howe: On the whole they look better sitting in than we would. But—well, let's pursue that and let's pick up Eli's suggestion for reorganization and see if we can get some comments in terms of pinpointing those points where racism seems to us most operative, and then in terms of doing something about it.

"Present allocation of federal and state funds to support public education tends to reinforce racial distinctions." I assume what is implied here is that there are differential levels of support where there are concentrations of disadvantaged people.

Kenneth Clark: This was one of the first points made in the discussion yesterday.

Thomas Pettigrew: I would like to spell out a second point which also backs the generalization, that is, it does this by giving grants to single districts—the point I tried to make yesterday—rather than incentives for cross-district . . .

Jerome Wiesner: Part of the old generalization, the rich get richer, the poor get poorer, as the suburbs pour more and more money into schools.

James Allen: I think that the problem is broader. It's really the present pattern of financing education which tends to reinforce racial distinctions; it's not just the allocation statement.

Clyde Ferguson: I think it's two separate things. First, it's the pattern of financing, which requires a certain kind of response in restructuring on a financial basis; then, once the financing is made available, the allocation of what is made available, also, and that's a separate and distinct problem; then what is made available that's in this allocation. . . .

James Allen: You see, I saw in the *New York Times* a few days ago that Con Edison is going to locate a tremendously big plant in New Rochelle and that New Rochelle people were saying, Now, this is great, we are going to be able to do all sorts of things with the new tax revenue. It's unfortunate that your pattern of financing education depends on this kind of chance location. That's the kind of thing I think you've got to get out of the way so that you can draw upon those resources and put the money where the need is.

Harold Howe: Doesn't this bring us back to the statement that, at the present time, the financing can and frequently does have racist effects or deny opportunity on a racial basis; and secondly, the positive recommendation that to correct this, we need new state equalization formulas, a decline in the local financial responsibility, and development of a federal equalization formula among states. These are the fine dimensions of this thing.

James Allen: Of course I would go farther than that, although I think you're more realistic. It seems to me that you really have got to take away the power to tax at the local level for education in order to get rid of these barriers that stand in the way of making educational decisions.

Franklin Roosevelt: I may be way out on a limb, but I think we need more than just equal allocation of funds and changing the pattern of financing. Maybe we need also sort of a Marshall Plan for some of the disadvantaged schools.

Jerome Wiesner: Well, that is really implied in some of these recommendations.

Franklin Roosevelt: I'm taking a point my friend Hubert Humphrey has been talking about. In Washington, D.C., we have schools where the teachers want to get out, not because of the problem of the children so much as the problem of the terrible facilities and the physical environment in which they have to work.

Jerome Wiesner: Well, Frank, let me read you a paragraph that is in our statement: "School construction financed by federal funds offers a way of resources. The schools bring black and white together and provide improved quality of education and so on. A new program to rebuild the schools of the central cities should bring the cities together with the suburbs to joint planning and use of facilities, provide special facilities for science, vocational, and a variety of other curricular areas which are far superior to those found in any usual city or suburb school." Maybe it doesn't say Marshall Plan, and maybe you need a special name for it, but the whole thrust of this paper is for a very major impact . . .

Franklin Roosevelt: Let me put it in its simplest terms. In the district I used to represent in Congress, there were two schools built in the Lincoln administration, and they were overcrowded by about 50 percent. They were firetraps. Actually these were integrated schools. But my concept is that even if you somehow or other join the West Side with Westchester in a school district, the Westchester kids just aren't going to want to go to that West Side school because of the poor facilities. And what I am saying is that we probably also need a massive approach to modernization of facilities for provision of science labs and other things.

Jerome Wiesner: That's what I read these paragraphs to be saying.

Franklin Roosevelt: It's not spelled out.

Harold Howe: I think that what you're adding to what we've already said is the idea that there needs to be—some people don't like the word—a compensatory program of financing. I think that's your Marshall Plan idea, which already exists in federal policy to some extent but does not exist very much in state policy.

James Allen: Well, the federal government does not have the restrictions, the inflexibility, that you have built into these state plans that have been developed for so long—and any time the legislature decides to increase state aid, it's got to assure that it builds on the same plan.

NEGRO INSTITUTIONS AND SHARED OR SEPARATE FACILITIES

Harold Howe: Let me take this same concept into higher education and ask what you do with it there. Should there be compensatory programs for institutions that have significant numbers of Negroes in their institutions, for institutions that are predominantly Negro, a compensatory arrangement for special financing so that they can jack up their facilities, and their instruction in the whole educational game? Again, should that be a part of this same recommendation?

Thomas Pettigrew: I'd like to put in a little qualification about facilities—not about other things. Facilities has a locking-in quality. Almost all of the predominantly Negro schools in the South are quite conveniently located to predominantly white schools. I'm picking up from a point Reverend Galamison made this morning. I do not believe that either set of those schools should get facilities' funds separately. It's a matter of economy for one thing, but that's not what motivates me.

Jerome Wiesner: I don't think that what you are saying is so.

Thomas Pettigrew: How do you mean?

Jerome Wiesner: If you take the eleven predominantly Negro schools, the eleven best Negro colleges, I don't think they are situated in such a way that they can all share in these facilities with white colleges. I don't think they should be required to either.

Thomas Pettigrew: I'm not talking in terms of requirements on *them*; I'm talking about requirements on the white schools, too.

Jerome Wiesner: Yes, but I think that the point was made this morning that these schools are so terribly important at this stage that you shouldn't sacrifice their primary role of education.

Kenneth Clark: Jerry, I think that if we keep that in mind, as clearly as you would like us to, you get right back to Gene Patterson's point. What I understand Tom is saying is that if we are going to make a statement about the use of federal funds for concrete facilities, are we going to ignore what was so clear in the area of public housing where you had a rhetoric, a verbalization, of integrated housing but instead you put up the facilities in part of the ghetto? You had only verbally integrated housing, and you had actually segregated housing. What Tom is saying is that if you are really serious about non-racially defined or constricted higher education . . . maybe it comes back to Gene's point. How serious are we about the nonsegregated problem in education, because there are strong and, I presume, realistic arguments to make the best of the existing segregated facilities, make them better. The United Negro College Fund argument is there, and it is easy to accept. What is difficult is what Tom has spoken for.

Jerome Wiesner: Well, maybe I don't understand his proposal.

Thomas Pettigrew: A library, for instance. I don't think Vanderbilt should get library-facilities money and Fisk federal money when they're there together.

Kenneth Clark: When they're duplicating library facilities.

Christopher Edley: I think we might be making the mistake of looking from the top down instead of from the bottom up. And at least it becomes simpler in my mind if I look from the bottom up.

I think the illustration is best in the public school context. As I see the public school system, it provides education, and students go to the trough and attempt to partake of this education. This education is uniform. The state dictates what's going to be taught in the classes each semester. This does not meet the individual needs. I am not aware of any public statement that says that the primary mission of education is to provide instruction that gives the individual the knowledge, the skills, that he needs to realize his potential. We have a public service concept in public education, and if it's provided in the school, the state and the localities have discharged their responsibilities. It's not their fault if the kids do not actually acquire the knowledge that is provided there. Now, it seems to me that starting on the lower level and thinking of this new education, we're no longer concerned with providing thirty-three kids in a class with the same instruction. We're concerned with reaching into the mind of each one of those individuals and giving him what he needs. Now. If we look at it in terms of need, then the finances, whether they are coming from the state or from the federal government, cannot be applied willy-nilly across the board; they cannot be apportioned on a per capita basis. They have to be allocated and reallocated on the basis of the needs. The needs would be greater in the ghetto. So we're looking up.

And the same thing would apply to colleges. And, therefore, the way federal and state resources are allocated has to be tied in with the individualized needs that we have now awakened to and are trying to meet. It seems to me that this solves some of the problem and it gives us, I hope, not too neat a formula— I certainly can't articulate the formula. But it deals on a reality basis; it allows for a differentiation between the varying needs. And I would suggest that you proceed in that direction.

James Allen: Then you can allocate resources: human resources, financial resources, material resources, and so on.

Kenneth Clark: I think that's a valuable formula in itself, but I still don't think it meets Gene Patterson and Tom Pettigrew's basic question, because the allocation of resources can reinforce a particular pattern and organizational system, and as Milt said this morning, we really don't know that a segregated school system is incapable of going beyond a certain quality of education. But if we take that path, we will be asking for an action commitment that will freeze the possibility of data coming in any other way.

Eugene Patterson: Yes, you are giving up your leverage over your suburban scholastic, that's the basic problem.

Kenneth Clark: That's right.

Jerome Wiesner: We're talking about higher education.

Kenneth Clark: It's even more clear in higher education, as long as you have what is really a dual, biracial system in a large area of this nation.

Jerome Wiesner: It seems to me you're saying nothing unless you get quite specific. You've got a system of Negro colleges with facilities that are poor by any standard you can apply to them, whose endowments are inadequate, whose funding for faculty are inadequate so that they cannot maintain good staffs. I think we would all agree; I think we *did* agree this morning that we should encourage the integration of these schools. But if you are going to set up a series of criteria for the granting of aid to these schools which makes it impossible for them to improve their facilities in any finite time, are we doing more good for the thousands of kids they're going to turn out in the next decade than if you do make it possible for them to make a quantum jump in the quality of their education relatively fast? I think this is the conflict.

Kenneth Clark: But Jerry, an equally relevant question would be, Could a particular form of financing perpetuate or reinforce the racist organization, or would another form of financing facilitate our movement toward the goal of integration?

Jerome Wiesner: I think that's a fair question. It's likely that anything that improves the quality of the institutions will also move us towards integration.

Christopher Edley: They're not necessarily mutually exclusive, Ken. It's possible—let's take Atlanta where there are a number of Negro colleges. Now, suppose in Atlanta there is a purely Negro college, and there is Emory. If we're allocating resources on the basis of need, Emory should get very little compared with the fourth- or fifth-rate Negro colleges, and I guess all of them in Atlanta are pretty good—maybe third-rate. Now, as we move the Negro college up on the basis of need to the level of Emory, we should be promoting integration of that school. But even if your point is that we should put policies into the dispensing of this money—if we say it's on the basis of need, and merely qualify that by saying that there will be added incentives for programs that promote integration, or programs that will help do away with racially isolated schools —it seems to me that you can still have the two things together in the funding recommendations.

Thomas Pettigrew: Let's be specific, though. Let's take Atlanta. Not Emory, which is where the North is. But Georgia State. It's right in the process at the moment of using major federal funds to expand. It's not geographically far from the Atlanta complex. Let's face it, Georgia put Georgia State in Atlanta to drain away what otherwise would have been a poor-white demand to go to some of the Atlanta Negro colleges. I mean this is being done in every Southern state. Building, snuggling up new state schools as close as you can, particularly in the cities, to the Negro colleges to prevent what happened in West Virginia naturally. And the federal government is party to this crime, in its present facilities. Now, the quickest way to further segregation in vested interests for the next two generations is to put money (and I'm not objecting to the other program) into facilities which stay there—bricks—and make these facilities separate. Now at some point you have to decide. I mean, you can't just say, It would be a great thing to integrate but we've got to put money into facilities that are separate. That's nice rhetoric.

Kenneth Clark: The Board of Education in the City of New York has been saying that for the last fourteen years.

Harold Howe: It seems to me we're saying exactly what you said, Tom, about the elementary and secondary schools, saying in statements we've already made here that school districts should be encouraged to get together, plan joint facilities, higher quality facilities, more efficient facilities, and yet we're not saying that only for that purpose will the federal government make money available. We're really saying that there will be a sweetener added, an equalization factor.

Harold Howe: The only thing we have got like this right now with colleges is Title III of the Higher Education Act, and the reason it's working this way is because we've turned it to this purpose, but we're not very successful with it. I think it would be very useful to have a statement in here that created some pressures, not an absolute requirement that separate institutions must get together, but some financial incentives to have them get together so that if they choose to remain separate, they pay a little price in this game of the federal dollar.

Christopher Edley: A question to Tom. Meharry is fighting like hell to hold on to its racial identity. It has so many white applicants, it's hard to get Negroes in. The same thing is happening at Howard University Medical School. It seems to me, there's no question that Howard is going to go the route of

West Virginia and that in fifteen or twenty years it will be a fifty-fifty school, if not a predominantly white school. Dean, you can comment on that. Howard is the prime example. Federal resources put in facilities that were primarily for the use of Negroes, but it's going to end up an integrated school, serving integrated purposes. So I wonder how you can be so sure that the predominantly Negro-school route of building up resources for the initial period will not result in those facilities falling into the integration stream a few years hence.

Thomas Pettigrew: Well, if they fall into the integration stream, I'd be delighted. It seems to me though that the burden of your comment is: Will the whites overrun these schools faster than Negroes are being absorbed into the white schools. That, it seems to me, you can, in fact, build in control for. All I am saying is a joint library, that doesn't throw more whites into the Atlanta complex, does it?

Jerome Wiesner: In the case of Meharry and Howard, the NIH [National Institutes of Health] has deliberately used its resources to build up those two medical schools. In a sense, whether you've legislated, whether you've written it down or not, pressures have been there to try to equalize the facilities.

Kenneth Clark: If we are very honest about Meharry and Howard, we will have to admit that they are being killed off precisely because sufficient numbers of Negro doctors have gotten medical training in other medical schools. And that all of the compensatory programs trying to make up for the deficit —the earlier educational deficit that would make it possible for them to be admitted on a single standard—so far have not resulted in a . . .

Christopher Edley: Don't limit it to medical schools. Don't limit it to medical schools.

Kenneth Clark: No, but I'm thinking just in terms of medical schools now. The consequences of this are found in the medical examination results, where Meharry and Howard are consistently at the bottom of the list of accredited medical schools in turning out doctors. This is a core problem of racism in American education. And I don't know, and I haven't yet been persuaded, that a perpetuation of this ameliorates racism.

Howard Howe: Should we or should we not recommend a system which encourages struggling institutions—and among them are going to be the predominantly Negro institutions— to develop cooperative arrangements with stronger institutions, which will be predominantly white institutions? Are there those who feel that we should not recommend such a thing?

Lisle Carter: I'm saying this sort of reluctantly. Somehow we have just sort of drifted into talking about this subject, and we've moved from higher education to talk of graduate education. Now I really submit this is the very lower end of the stick of the problems we are dealing with here, and we just can't seem to get any priorities focused here. We had some experimentation in predominantly Negro schools or weaker schools tying in with others, and frankly I don't think the evidence is very good that the weaker schools got much out of the experiment.

Thomas Pettigrew: Yes, that's precisely the kind of thing I am against because that is patronizing and paternalistic in its very substance.

Eugene Patterson: Mr. Chairman, doesn't this come back to that matter of priorities that I raised earlier? We're all for compensatory education and we're all for integrated education. We're for both. It's a matter of priorities. Is it impossible to phrase a resolution in favor of such a Marshall Plan as this:

a plan that places our priority on ultimate integration, leaving the guidelines in your hands, if necessary, to force and push and cajole the schools in the direction Ken and Tom are talking about, which I devoutly believe has got to be pressed forward with the use of the federal government.

Harold Howe: The only new issue we have in this conversation is whether construction should be used in this way. Already, operating funds in a great variety of ways have been so used. Tom introduced a new issue: Doesn't construction freeze in place a segregated arrangement?

Kenneth Clark: This certainly seems to be a very important question.

Eugene Patterson: Awfully important in the public school situation where you have a clear choice. You're going to build an education park; you're going to build a ghetto school.

Christopher Edley: On construction, I think that the best that you can hope to do is to follow the language in the urban renewal legislation. This language was conceived in '49 and, as modified, says roughly that you must promote integration. Now we all know that in public housing and urban renewal projects this mandate, to promote integration, has not succeeded very well, but it has given the Administration the excuse and justification for pushing for a degree of integration. Now, if in this proposal you say that it will promote integration, it seems to me that is the most you're going to get out of it. I don't know of any way you can spell it out to make the administrators honestly and sincerely do it and enforce it down the line. We can try for that. But I don't see any point in agonizing over how you do it. You merely put in that there is nothing special about education. The federal funds have to be spent on a nondiscriminatory basis to start with. If the funds are being used to perpetuate segregated education, it's illegal and unconstitutional to start with. You are just putting in an affirmative statement. At least I *hope* you agree with me that if you try to administer the funds so as to build up segregated education, that the excluded group can file a suit and stop you in your tracks.

Harold Howe: You have to remember that a predominantly Negro college is not in the eyes of the law a segregated institution, and therefore, buildings can be built there perfectly legally. It is a segregated institution in fact, but not in law, and that is why we have an issue, I think.

Lisle Carter: What you're really calling for is the kind of regional planning in higher education that we are moving toward in other fields. We don't have that kind of sharing of our developmental facilities and so forth now—at least not enforced by federal policy. If we balanced the needs of the higher educational institutions in the metropolitan area, the region, or whatever it is, that would imply that you're going to get a mix of students throughout the system because, in order to have that kind of balanced planning, you're going to go to the strongest institution to get the particular service that is needed.

Harold Howe: Let me try to state the proposition in another way. Is there anybody who objects to including in this recommendation the idea that weaker institutions need general support from the federal government for both operations and buildings, and that there should be some premium placed on the funds they get for those purposes if they will reach for planning with other institutions as that can be arranged. It's this kind of thing you are talking about, Lisle. In other words, an isolated institution may have no other choice but to go it alone, but there are going to be situations when many won't have to. And this as a general proposition would be useful, unless there is major objection.

Clyde Ferguson: The problem is really not weaker and stronger institutions as such. The problem is black institutions and famous institutions. That's what the problem is.

Harold Howe: You can't get a federal statute enacted for black institutions.

Clyde Ferguson: No, you can't use those words, but you can get a federal statute enacted which is going to put money in that particular place.

Harold Howe: We already have one called the Developing Institutions Act, and we have spent thirty million dollars a year for this purpose. We're talking about moving that into construction, something that's never been done. A few of the state planning agencies for construction are doing the kind of thing Lisle is talking about. They get into a lot of trouble about it. I think it would be a very useful thing to try to include this concept; I quite agree with your point that the predominantly Negro colleges ought to get first consideration in this, as indeed they do under the Developing Institutions Act.

Clyde Ferguson: Yes, for function of this particular body, which is not the legislature and is not bound by the Constitution. Though we don't recommend unconstitutional actions, we ought to say exactly what we think in terms of the problem and leave it to the legislators and the Department of Justice to use "developing" or "weaker than weak" and proper statutory language.

Harold Howe: I'll buy that.

Jerome Wiesner: There is a conflict among us. I think Ken and Tom are saying they don't want to do this.

Lisle Carter: They don't want to strengthen the weaker black institutions?

Thomas Pettigrew: It's how you do it.

Kenneth Clark: The problem is not that simple.

Jerome Wiesner: I think that's what it amounts to, in fact.

Kenneth Clark: Now Jerry, let's not run away with this. Milt this morning raised the question of helping to clarify what we meant by elimination of Negro colleges. If one wanted to eliminate Negro colleges the way one eliminates white colleges, then what Tom and I are saying is that federal financing should facilitate that rather than reinforce the polarization.

Kenneth Boulding: I must say I think there's a real problem, a difference of opinion here, because if you're going to eliminate the Negro colleges, you're going to eliminate the Catholic colleges, you're going to eliminate Brandeis—you see, there's something here which doesn't come out somehow. That is that, well, it's a question of what I call a mosaic pattern of a society. That is, Are we? Is this what we want? The thing that is wrong with segregation is its compulsory quality. It seems to me that voluntary segregation has a lot to be said for it in many fields. There are many Jewish schools. There's no reason why you can't have Negro schools in exactly this sense, if this is needed to give a sense of identity. I've always felt, ever since I taught at Fisk for a year, that the great problem with the Negro in this country is that he's an American and practically nothing else. You see, all the rest of us are hyphenated. Whereas the Negro has been here so long, really, that he's just an American. There's a feeling now that the Negro has got to become an Irishman or something. It's a whole lot of tomfoolery. Here is this demand—an identity, a piece within the mosaic. Instead of being all this damn cement, you see. The Negro's tired of just being cement. I think he's quite right about this and that there's something we haven't been listening to here.

Jerome Wiesner: It's gravel.

Kenneth Boulding: It's gravel! And somehow, this isn't in our mythology at the moment. This is why I see a lot in the position that integration has become a kind of substitute idea for what we are really getting at. If we mix up the race problem and the poverty problem, we're going to mess them both up.

The thing one learns from the history of this country is that if you try to do things for the poor by identifying the poor as X, in doing something for X, you end up doing it for the rich. It always happens. On the whole, our social policy in this country is the policy of subsidizing the rich under the guise of helping the poor. Agricultural policy is a prize example of this. Mr. What's-his-name in the Senate gets a hundred-and-fifty-thousand-dollar check, you see, for not planting cotton—and it's the same with education. Look at our state universities. The state universities are scandalous subsidies to the rich. In the University of Michigan, the students were from families in the top 10 percent of the income bracket, and they're quite heavily subsidized. There's no sense in this at all. The same with public education. If you make education free and good it's the rich who will take advantage of it. Any time you do anything for X, whoever he is, whether a farmer or a Negro or anything, it will be the rich, Negro or white, who will cop it. Somehow this assumption that poverty and racism can be run together isn't true.

RACE AND TEACHER TRAINING

Kenneth Boulding: The more I've been thinking about racism today, the more it seems to me that, in a sense, rather scientific education almost has to be the answer to this. Racism arises out of folk biology, doesn't it? All this stuff about blood and whatnot. Whereas the slightest knowledge of genetics destroys all your confidence in your ancestors. Most of the people in this country don't realize how the genetic theory, which is very recent, after all, has completely blown to hell all our notions about family and being proud of being Joneses or something. Also, the fact that racial differences are primarily cultural, not very well based on genetics. Your skin may be black but your skeleton's as white as mine; these genetic differences, which are practically real, are essentially superficial. This is what we are trying to say all the time here, and I think somehow we have to reiterate this, that the real enemy of racism is biology and nothing else. The thing that keeps racism alive is the fact that we don't teach it and that hence false knowledge of race just gets perpetuated from generation to generation. I'd like to know how many people in this country understand genetic theory. Even remotely. I'd be surprised if it is more than 2 percent.

I hope you begin the document by just one sentence which shows there is only one race—and that is the human race. There, you see, there it is, and this biologically is true. And then I hope we can say that differentiations are not terribly bad. You see it isn't a bad thing to be different from other people. In a sense, there's a great deal to be said for preserving this marvelous variety of the human race; if we can invent some green people I think that would be marvelous. There's a color missing in the human spectrum. Somehow we got to say this: we don't have to end up all uniform.

Harold Howe: It seems to me it's just this kind of statement that perhaps says to us that the most useful record of this meeting is going to be a few quotations taken from the tape rather than things agreed upon. I would remind you that when I went to get a driving license down South a few years ago, I entered on the sheet where it has race, "human," and they wouldn't accept it. Well, let's not get hung up any more on the Negro colleges.

The next statement to deal with is that the quality of education provided for American children differs according to their racial, social, and economic status. Now, outside of economic and taxation and fiscal enterprises of the federal, state, and local governments, which we've been discussing, what kinds of approaches do we make to this particular problem?

Kenneth Clark: Like Roosevelt's suggestion of a Marshall Plan.

Harold Howe: Would you be willing to include here this notion of a number of very large-scale major demonstrations across the country? Do you think this is a useful idea?

Unidentified: Yes, I do.

Harold Howe: Would you be willing to include really significant changes in teacher training?

Unidentified: Yes.

Jerome Wiesner: In connection with that, it seems to me important to stress availability of funds for experimentation in teacher training, which is implicit but I think not as explicit as we ought to make it.

Franklin Roosevelt: Maybe you should pull in here some of the scattered incentives for higher teacher performance, as well as incentives for students, and perhaps an expansion of the National Defense Scholarship concept in areas to assist racially, economically, and socially deprived kids on their way up to college level.

Jerome Wiesner: In connection with teacher training, as you call it, I would like once again to call for a federally sponsored program of institutes rather than institutes run by the school systems. I think that alternative routes for teachers who have an opportunity to study these problems certainly would be very useful, because there will be systems which won't make the kind of changes we want—won't open the opportunities.

Harold Howe: This is the experience of people who try to introduce new curriculum in the schools—unless you do something about teacher training aspects, you're lost. You can produce a lot of new printed material, and it will be filed away or used the way the old material was used as a substitute for the old and not make any difference.

Milton Galamison: Are we, Mr. Chairman, in the teacher training aspect, calling for certain kinds of clinical experience for teachers?

Harold Howe: We say we need more course background in anthropology and other such areas—psychology, sociology—and secondly, much deeper exposure to the actual problems the person will confront in the classroom during the process of training. That's all we say.

Milton Galamison: I am becoming more and more convinced as I move along that this problem can't be modified in the classroom—that no matter how much reading and no matter how much teaching in terms of Negro history and all that sort of thing a teacher is exposed to, the real vacuum in this whole procedure is the living experience of the teacher. And while we look with misgiving at the South, we have equal barriers, if not more insuperable barriers, in the North to real communication between black and white people. We rely on geographical separation to keep races separated. My whole argument is that you can't possibly be fair to people you don't know. In this whole structure most white people don't really know black people. Further, a principal-parent relationship is not an equal relationship, a teacher-child relationship is not an equal relationship, so you never get the living experience. Now the thing that amazes me is that some of our universities will develop these year-abroad programs and send students to Asia and Africa to get to know black people. They never think of sending students to Harlem, where they could get a living experience. I think that much of the attitudinal problem that we face and much of the ethnocentric gap that we need to bridge could be resolved if we had more clinical exposure for teachers in the kind of atmosphere where they're going to be teaching. I would recommend this strongly, with any kind of training programs.

Franklin Roosevelt: Milton, yesterday, before you came, I think, I mentioned my feeling that we ought to have more field training for the teacher during the study years. And what you were just saying about the year abroad ties in a bit with what both Eli Ginzberg and I mentioned about the participation of the college student and the high school student in the community educational system surrounding the college.

Erik Erikson: Where would you get the people who would train the teachers, and the textbooks which would help to teach them to do this? I agree with you entirely but I think some preliminary steps are necessary, and I don't know exactly where this belongs here. I should think it would be something that one should think of under every item, once you think about the whole question of changing attitudes. But it looks to me as though a whole corps of people would need to be trained. Clinical is not enough, you see. I know how you mean clinical, and I like the word, but clinical for most people means a question of pathology.

Jerome Wiesner: You do this best, I think, in the context of curriculum reform, so that people are involved in trying to learn a new substantive basis for their teaching at the same time they're getting these other "experiences" and inputs. This means you have to build up a massive system. You first have to develop your curriculum materials, then you have to build up what economists would call the infrastructure, I suppose, for the dissemination of the information. In the case of the new science courses which we've propagated over the last decade we've done it that way. We've had massive development programs involving teachers in the schools as well as specialists in curriculum development, material development, making the courses, and then you fanned out to a very large number of teacher training institutes—there are many of them in every state—federally supported. You tried to get the teachers to understand the new material. And, I think, in that context you probably would be more successful than if you brought teachers into an institute structured and designed to try to change their attitudes. I think that once you say that is what you're trying to do, you'll kill the thing.

Erik Erikson: You see, when you do something like your science program, you have already established what the difficulties in understanding are. What is ignorance? What is difficult to comprehend? By what message can you quickly change this? When it comes to what you're talking about now—the resistance to meeting people and understanding them—this is simply not as well defined as that kind of ignorance.

Jerome Wiesner: I understand. But you still have to try. For one high school physics course, we spent about ten million dollars in developmental material. I doubt whether a tenth of that sum had ever been spent trying to develop new approaches to the problem we're talking about here in curriculum materials.

Donald Ogilvie: I wanted to argue that many of the students in colleges have been talking about revision of curriculum in terms of black studies; meaning, in effect, incorporation into curriculum offerings courses dealing with black experience both in the American context and the foreign context. Where are examples of these courses; where are the people to teach them? There are examples of the courses. There are some people teaching them but not enough. And perhaps what is necessary is some sponsorship, either federal or possibly foundation, to get some of these people together to draw up perhaps a model curriculum for each of the several levels of education, primary through collegiate.

Harold Howe: I think this is a good suggestion. Let me suggest, also, that there is a tremendous backlog. The teachers now in the schools are going to be there, on the average, for twenty-five years; there's a massive program necessary to do a catch-up job. I don't know to what extent it's realistic to think you can change attitudes and practices of that group of people. But it's worth a try, and it would seem to me that our recommendation ought to include the idea that, either through state or federal support, there should be every fifth year a real, defined catch-up process. It will be expensive and it will increase the staff of the schools by one-fifth in order to make it happen. But you need this sort of massive move in order to get at the problem, at least in areas of concentration of need.

Jerome Wiesner: Now there is one very simple economic incentive that has been used successfully in the science programs, and I think it would work here. Teachers are traditionally underpaid; teachers generally don't have a lot to do in the summertime. The National Science Foundation summer institute actually *pays* them to participate in those programs.

Milton Galamison: This is what we recommended last summer in District Thirteen—that federal funds which were available be used to sponsor some kind of summer institute for teachers who would come and live in the ghetto for six weeks. *Live* there. Set the schools up as dormitories, use the cafeteria to feed teachers and then let these teachers be exposed constantly in the afternoon and evening to the kind of thing that Mr. Ogilvie is talking about in terms of academic material. But in the daytime to work around in the community with day camps or with pastors or just with the ongoing life of the community. This would be not to change anybody's attitude drastically, don't misunderstand me. It wouldn't do that for everyone, but it would certainly modify and condition some of the more negative attitudes that make it so difficult to get a teacher to function in the community. But the program never materialized.

Donald Ogilvie: I would add to that—again trying to get back to curriculum because I think it's so important—that if the teacher remains hostile to the student, the child can identify that. Often this is personalized. Educational materials the child is fed in school only corroborate that negative impression. There is nothing to replace it—the child can't go beyond the teacher and the text to the truth.

Erik Erikson: Wouldn't it therefore be rather important that at least a few teachers who are gifted in some way learn to recognize hostile attitudes which they didn't know they had? One might despair if one asks how to teach a whole generation of teachers. But I think that one shouldn't overlook the importance of a few good teachers learning that for themselves.

Jerome Wiesner: I wonder if we shouldn't talk about the administrative principals and superintendents, who have a terribly important role.

Harold Howe: Obviously, all educational personnel. I remind you that the legislative vehicle to do the kind of things we're talking about is in existence. It's the Educational Development

Act, passed a year ago. You can even train college presidents with it if you choose to do so. It's a broad piece of legislation with all kinds of authority in it to provide these institutes that Jerry talks about, to do them differently, to run them for a full year if that makes sense, to include principals and superintendents, etc., etc. So it's a question of money, policy, and imagination rather than new legislation to do all these things we've been talking about for twenty minutes.

Jerome Wiesner: Then maybe we could stress the need to do it.

EVALUATION OF TEACHER PERFORMANCE

Harold Howe: As I look at the systems that exist in good colleges and universities for selection of personnel, that is, for promotion and selection, the senior faculty members, by and large, decide who is going to be a junior faculty member and whether he's going to get to be a senior one. There is nothing analogous in the schools. There is a great unwillingness in the schools to assume that kind of responsibility. Teachers shun it, yet it's always seemed to me possible to consider and to develop some real experiments in having a much broader kind of faculty responsibility in the schools for differentiating among teachers, thinking about what assignments they should have and for including this idea of achievement as one of the components that would help with those judgments. In the university, achievement of the students does not enter into those judgments very much, I don't suppose. Probably they look at a man's graduate students and how they get along and that sort of thing. They look at his research; they certainly look at his teaching; there's evidence that colleges and universities are generally trying to do more of that. I'm wondering whether a recommendation connected in part to student achievement, as well as to the other factors to which faculty members will be sensitive, would be useful.

Jerome Wiesner: Faculty responsibility for development of the faculty essentially. It is difficult to do this in the face of the union problems in most states, where unions are becoming stronger, and where the notion of any kind of merit recognition is almost anathema. It's something one really ought to pay attention to.

James Allen: We're moving in a direction related to this in New York in trying to work toward licensing and certification based on performance. That is, the university or teacher training institution would certify to us that they prepared the teachers in science or some field, and we would give them a provisional license but not a permanent license until we have some kind of a performance test which might include achievement and many other things.

Harry Rowen: How would this performance be measured?

James Allen: Well, we haven't gotten that far yet, but the concept is that the university that prepared the teacher—the teacher training institution—and the local school system would work out an assessment or appraisal plan for three or four years of the teacher's work on the job and on the basis of that would then recommend to the state that the teacher be given a certificate, a permanent license to continue teaching or not. It would be under some supervision from those that helped prepare the teacher, but would help the teacher's peers, experienced people in the school system, make a judgment as to whether or not that teacher should be continued as a licensed teacher.

Kenneth Clark: Is this periodic evaluation or just random selection?

James Allen: Well, we haven't carried it that far. I would hope that we could do it periodically, but I think we're going to have a hard time selling it this way. We're planning to move. Let me put it this way: we're planning to move from the old system of licensing and certifying teachers by counting courses and all that sort of stuff. Say to the university, You certify to us that you're satisfied that under some kind of an all-university arrangement a teacher is prepared to teach. We'll give a provisional license, but we won't give a permanent license until we've got some judgment of the performance on the job.

Franklin Roosevelt: Can I ask, Milton, how does this fit into some of the ideas that are coming to the fore in decentralization, where the community is going to want to have a voice in assessing the ability of the teacher to teach?

Milton Galamison: I really ought to defer to Ken here. No, I have no particular method to recommend for evaluation. I'm not an expert in that field. But it is presumed that in a community-controlled situation in a decentralized system there would be an evaluation of teachers. Now, it's assumed that teachers would participate in this evaluation themselves, but also that the lay people who would help with the evaluation would bring in consultants, if necessary, so that some fairly uniform objective procedure for evaluating teachers would be possible—but the exact formula, I just wouldn't know.

Kenneth Clark: I think that part of the confusion which gives rise to racial tension is the belief that that incident in Ocean Hill–Brownsville was one in which lay parents suddenly and arbitrarily decided to get rid of nineteen teachers. This is not the case. The person who made that decision was a professional. Everyone forgets that.

If you use the model example of colleges and universities, it *seems* that you do not have a system for differential rewards, but in fact you *do*, by virtue of promotion—you know, rank. You don't have anything comparable to rank in elementary and secondary schools. I understand that Massachusetts recently passed some legislation with ranks for teachers, four ranks. Now maybe we can get around the bugaboo of no merit pay by developing some system of graduated levels from entering levels to master teacher and beyond, and a range of salary within those.

Jerome Wiesner: One of the important things I think that you'd want to achieve by decentralization is what the smaller communities do have now—namely, the administrative people in the school system are responsive to the attitudes of the parents, the school committee. You don't have that in New York City, presumably. You have an administrator you have confidence in, and you *back* him in dealing with the teachers. It's the lack of that ability to have any communication with the people who are running the schools that is at the heart of the problem you are talking about.

Harold Howe: I would be very friendly to the idea of differentiation among staff on the basis of some rational judgments about their performance in producing excellence in the classroom, and it seems to me that the only person who can make that judgment is probably staff itself, after the university model. I'd buy Ken's notion of a hierarchy in the public school staff. I realize quite well that the professional won't buy it, but it ought to be tried.

Kenneth Clark: In Massachusetts, oddly enough, the union didn't argue against it.

Harold Howe: I made a speech on this subject to the AFT [American Federation of Teachers] Convention about a year and a half ago, and I pretty near got run out of the city. I think it's well worth keeping on the agenda.

C. Vann Woodward: I've been thinking about this comparison. As you know the promotional power of the university faculties—and the faculty rights or prerogatives in these matters—is always much under attack, now from the alumni, from the pressure groups, now from the students. The students want to get into the act, and they want to vote on promotion and appointments and all this. This is a highly professional group with a sense of professional identity that I think has been carried too far in the matter of tenure. I don't know whether my colleagues would agree, but I would certainly not want to slip into our recommendations a tenure system such as the universities have. I'm skeptical of it at this time.

Unidentified: You already have it. Public schools have it.

Harold Howe: It's a lot more vicious in the public schools, it happens sooner; and there is no disciplined examination really, except once after three years, in most places.

Jerome Wiesner: A thing to remember about the university structure is that the hardest thing to measure and the thing that is least measured is promotion of its teachers. It is an extremely difficult thing even in a well-organized university.

Leo McLaughlin: I'd say the students should be consulted. I think they're the only ones who really know whether there is any teaching going on. You know this business about the other members of the faculty making the judgment. I tried for twelve years to evaluate teachers at the college level, and I failed. I could tell you the very good teachers, and I could tell you the really bad teachers, but that does not make up for more than about 15 percent of the total, and the ability of the large majority of them was absolutely unknown to me. This is why I think student evaluation is a very important element. The students aren't kidding around about it.

Harold Howe: Are you talking about this in the school or in the university?

Leo McLaughlin: I can't talk about it in the schools at all. I know just the college or university.

Clyde Ferguson: The parent is at least one step removed, and you can learn a lot about what goes on in the classroom by talking to your kids when they come back.

ROLE OF TEACHERS' UNIONS

Christopher Edley: A number of unkind things have been said about teachers' unions. I certainly have tried to say some of them myself. Now I wonder if it's possible for this group to make a statement with reference to school unions. Can we say that they've carried tenure too far, or can we say that, in many instances, they tend, to use my words, to become the enemy of the people. You can say it any way you want to, but it seems to me that for the length and breadth of this country no one is saying that the union in New York has gone too far. During my time in Philadelphia the union there went too far. And it was standing in the way of improving education for minority groups. I think it would be a very courageous and forward-looking thing if a group with the prestige of the individuals here, excluding myself, could go on record making a critical statement concerning the wrongdoings of the unions.

James Allen: As a minimum we could say that we have concerns here that what the unions have built into their structure and their procedures are the very same things that they've been fighting in the bureaucracy.

Harold Howe: Well, I think we could say a couple of things. I don't know whether the kinds of general criticism you suggest ought to be made, but I think it could be said, and I'd like the New York people with direct experience to see if they could document this, that the kinds of contracts teachers are negotiating with cities, and the seniority provisions of those contracts, and all the energy that goes into arranging those seem to me to have two effects. One is to place the professional organizations almost entirely in the camp of self-interest, only paying lip service to educational improvement. And secondly to create arrangements which do filter out the senior elements of the least desirable schools and leave a higher-turnover staff and less-experienced group in the more difficult schools. Is that fair to say?

James Allen: I think much more examination of the situation in a place like New York would have to be made before you can make a judgment. I think there are an awful lot of plusses, too, in what the unions have been able to accomplish, but . . .

Kenneth Clark: Including quality of education?

James Allen: Well, in getting some of the things that we think help to improve the quality of education.

Unidentified: Higher salaries.

Kenneth Clark: But higher salaries not in any way tied to performance.

James Allen: Well, I'm not defending it; all I'm saying is that I think we ought to remember the number of plusses that the union brings about because the teachers have found a way to have a voice, a much more effective voice.

Elinor Gordon: But the voice keeps the bureaucracy in a city like New York going, and there's a hoax going on among many of the programs which are supposed to be Higher Horizon programs.

Harold Howe: More Effective Schools.

Elinor Gordon: More Effective Schools, and they're a hoax. They're paper work. And they're not improving education. I don't know if we should say something about the unions.

James Allen: Well, we have More Effective Schools there and, they tell me, they look a lot better than some others that I've been in.

Lisle Carter: Could we have a statement on the blockages to change, the extent to which unions contribute to those blockages, in part intentionally, and in part in fact? Because you're talking about deficits in the schools, and it seems to me this has not been adequately discussed.

Erik Erikson: I can see how you would want to talk about rewards, but do you want to talk about penalties?

Kenneth Clark: You can take out "penalties."

Erik Erikson: You see, what happens in academic circles is that if somebody is judged not to come up to standards, he is permitted to go somewhere else. Very rarely is anybody penalized or removed. He's just not reappointed, and he takes a position somewhere else. Isn't that so?

Kenneth Clark: In the State Department they call it "selection out" and academics call it "up or out."

Erik Erikson: But now, since you have discussed the clinical improvement of attitudes, is there any agency that could judge a teacher's performance and make suggestions as to what exactly is wrong with it and what could be improved, or is it just a matter of getting the reward or being removed?

Kenneth Clark: That is supposed to be the responsibility of the supervisors, the principals, and the superintendents. But that is rarely, if ever, exercised.

Erik Erikson: Would the unions cooperate with the program?

Christopher Edley: Their basic position is that they will protect the teachers. You talk about moving teachers or penalizing them or doing anything that would affect them or hurt them in a negative way. *Now* the unions are not going to play ball.

Erik Erikson: Not to improve the teachers. That's not their function.

Kenneth Clark: For example, in Ocean Hill–Brownsville the union is on record as protecting the right of any teacher to initiate a transfer from a school without regard to need. That same union pulled out a hundred and thirty teachers because the administrators of that school district decided that certain teachers should be transferred. The union has been excellent. In fact, I think that Albert Shanker is one of the most effective union leaders on the New York City scene now in protecting the interests of teachers, because they have their cake and eat it too. They provide protection for the teachers while the public, parents, and students have really no protection under this theory of allocation of teachers.

Harold Howe: Ken, I think we have got to be careful not to act as if all of the United States was New York City. There is, you know, a danger there, because there are many, many other kinds of problems in lots of other places.

Kenneth Clark: I was just answering Erik's question on the role of the unions and what you can expect from them.

EDUCATIONAL RIGIDITIES AND NEW ALTERNATIVES

Harold Howe: Jim, let me ask you a question. How do you feel about the possibility of having a much more open market for educational leadership in the schools that exist. Do you think this is a viable thing to reach for? By this I mean that —not in your state, but in many states—there are rather restrictive arrangements about who shall be a school superintendent. There are typically no such arrangements about who shall be the head of a junior college. They look around, find somebody they think who might do the job, and get away with it. And yet in the schools there tend to be rather restrictive arrangements. There are many, many possible sources for executives in schools, and the business world is not the least of them. I just wonder whether we ought to open up this thing and at least see the experimentation in this area rather than assuming that the groups by which educational leadership is created make sense.

James Allen: I would urge it. You know we've been trying to do it.

Jerome Wiesner: You have to be very careful, because one of the reasons we have these things is to protect the schools. With the system we have of local economy there is always a great danger that the school committee, the school boards of rather limited experience and even limited good will, will put people in there for political reasons or reasons other than educational accomplishment. Sure, there are a lot of restrictions which maybe look a little silly, but they do tie the hands of people who would do bad things. And one has to be careful not to open a Pandora's box.

Harold Howe: Right.

Kenneth Clark: Jerry, isn't it true, though, that most of the things we are now looking upon as barriers or abuses or rigidities were initiated as basis for reform?

Jerome Wiesner: Yes, but they still function as important controls in key places and, in the guise of reform, you have to be sure you don't free as many new evils as you do reforms.

Kenneth Clark: Such as the earlier reforms that have become the evils we are addressing ourselves to.

Christopher Edley: I have a sentence, about the policy or philosophy that is behind public education today, that says: "The high summation of public education is to impart instruction which enables each student to realize his intellectual and vocational potential." And if my hunch is right, that sentence is revolutionary, because education is not afforded in public schools today on the basis of realizing the potential of the individual. It's dispensed on a uniform basis, and I want to make sure I get it in the record in its entirety.

Harold Howe: Well, I think we should get it in. I would say that doing what the sentence says is revolutionary.

Christopher Edley: I agree with that.

Harold Howe: The real problem is that there has been lip service to that sentence and no action.

Christopher Edley: My experience has been that as you try to do innovative things in the school system, you run into yesterday's philosophy that you provide the same subject matter here and there regardless of the individual needs of those kids. As long as that philosophy is rampant, we're going to have difficulty getting reform, because the teachers and the supervisors don't believe in this simple statement.

Kenneth Clark: They are much more subtle and smooth than that. They claim belief in that statement but then define the potential of each child in terms of his economic status. I say this out of fifteen years of constant dialogue—not controversy but dialogue—with these people. They will repeat this more frequently than anything else, but then impose upon the child what Ken Boulding calls their folk genetics or their folk cultural anthropology and think they know that this child has no greater potential.

Lisle Carter: I'd like to ask a question—and it still reflects my trouble with where and how we're going here. And the question is, Assuming that we had the will that Elinor Gordon asked about earlier, where would we like to see the educational system in five years, and ten years? I mean what would be different about it? What would be realizable, assuming that we had the will to do it, and of course commit the resources to do it? Where are we trying to go?

Jerome Wiesner: One of the things I said yesterday was that I think we should complement our statement by offering real alternate opportunities, suggesting two ways of implementing it. One was to have other educational means, not as a threat but as an optional educational opportunity.

Franklin Roosevelt: There's one danger here that we've got to keep in mind. And that is that the alternative, which I assume would be financed through some scholarship concept, will attract the students with the higher potential, and the public school is likely to wind up with the dregs.

Jerome Wiesner: I didn't say that there should be an alternative to public schools. You know, it's conceivable that you could have more than one public school system in a major big city. . . . And secondly, as an alternative, people have been talking about the possibility of providing tuition aid for students to go to other schools, including private school systems, and I think that has some merit. In the long run you may not like it, but when you're dealing with the kind of frozen situation that we have today, I think that you have to use every expedient to break it. And I think one way of breaking it quickly is to give the parents the opportunity and the funds, the support, to choose where their kids go to school.

Franklin Roosevelt: Let me once again be the devil's advocate. This happened in the state of Virginia as a device to evade the integration program, and God, let's not *us* get on the record by any implication that we're supporting that kind of thing.

Jerome Wiesner: Well, we're not supporting that kind of thing.

Unidentified: What would be the safeguard against it?

Kenneth Clark: You wouldn't be able to make that recommendation without at the same time making a safeguard.

Jerome Wiesner: You can certify the institutions . . .

Eugene Patterson: What would be the purpose of this competition?

Jerome Wiesner: The first purpose would be to give an option to get good education now. This is not competition. This is an alternative route. I'm suggesting there might be several alternative routes, one of them being a publicly financed alternative school system of a substantial size. The second route might be to allow for alternate institutes where they could go to school. In New York City, they might choose to go to Fieldston.

Kenneth Clark: Suppose they choose the parochial schools, as most youngsters in Harlem and other ghettos do in order to get a better break? What would you think of the problem there? The kids who grow up in Harlem can't afford the higher-priced private schools.

Clyde Ferguson: Nobody turns the children away.

Christopher Edley: I think this has been taken out of context. I assume that you mean alternatives bigger and better than some we have already experimented with, and so far these have been programs like the Street Academy, programs that have been designed for the losers in the system. We've also done a great deal of talking about model schools and alternatives. I've been on this kick for six or seven years, putting in alternatives to compete, but we always had to show the public school system how it can be done, that it can be done. O.K. Now I want to go on record. I can't go along with a long-range program that would eliminate the concept of the public school or a system where the bulk of the kids would be educated in something other than a nonpublic school. I'm willing to demonstrate that better education can be accomplished and to show by competitive comparison to the school system that it is failing in a job that can be done. . . .

Jerome Wiesner: Let me show you one form that it could take. We're talking about decentralizing the New York school system. It could decentralize all the way to the point where the individual school is getting appropriate funds. You could then say that the schoolchildren didn't have to go to the school district in which they lived. This would give you a tremendous number of opportunities in New York City, and you would still be in the public school system.

Christopher Edley: But let me tell you what you're doing, what you're saying. You're saying that we need flexibility to carry on this type of experimentation—fine—and you know if these things are successful, I will be one of the first to say, let's institutionalize them and make them applicable across the board. But I'm not going to say institutionalize them now— not knowing whether the results are going to be fine. I think that decentralization is fine in three or four schools; I think it's fine in a dozen schools. But I am not ready to decentralize from the Atlantic seaboard to the Pacific at this point until I find out whether it works in New York City or whether it works in New York State.

Harold Howe: You're looking for parental and pupil choice.

Jerome Wiesner: It is my hope that this system evolves to be permanent.

Clyde Ferguson: It's not just an interim arrangement to re-form the public school system.

Jerome Wiesner: I think that the thing that is basically wrong with public education in the United States is that there is no choice and there is no competition. And I think this is just as true for the teachers. One of the reasons the university system has strength is that if a professor doesn't like teaching at Harvard, he can go to Princeton, and there is competition for teachers.

Unidentified: That's going up?

Harold Howe: I'm not sure that's a good analysis.

CHANGING THE CLIMATE OF PREJUDICE

Bruno Bitker: I don't want the meeting to break up, Mr. Chairman, without getting back to the fact that this is to be an action report—and the fact that it will go to the President of the United States from the President's Commission. Now, all of what I've been hearing the last couple of days is, of course, intended for educators, and I don't feel qualified to pass on any of these questions. I'm for everything that has been said here today by way of improvement of education. But let me say that I do not think that what has been said here, if I may say this with due apologies, has been directed solely to educational reform. The conference was intended to get *action* on the American scene in education—to break down racial prejudice. All we've done is talk about how to improve teachers or how you get better schools or how you decentralize or how you draw up the funds better or you give control to the federal government instead of state or local governments.

I don't know how many of you are familiar with this document. This is a statement on race and prejudice. It's a UNESCO statement. Surprisingly enough—perhaps not so surprising—this statement of UNESCO issued last September was made as a result of a conference in Paris by some of the world's most informed persons on this question, including our colleague here today, Dean Ferguson. The surprising part about it is that no recognized or responsible educational agency in the United States since last September—correct me if I'm wrong about this, Dean—has so much as acknowledged the existence of this document, although it's obviously basic. It says in more words what Ken Boulding referred to so well—biology. It discusses it in more scientific terms, but I think this conference ought to get to the race question in some way and at least ought to end up by either approving or disapproving this statement.

The other thing is that I think our problem is not how to better the teachers or how to educate the teachers. I'm all for this. Our problem is how do you sell the soap. I used the example, yesterday, of cigarettes because it was so obvious that if you can sell cigarettes against the Surgeon General's report that it is bad for health, you ought to be able to sell something as basic as the American principle of equality. I would be very disappointed if out of this conference did not come *some kind* of a consensus on *how you persuade the American people to support Americans.* It's just so simple. How do you sell the soap?

Harold Howe: I think you find major agreement around this table to the very good principle set forth in that statement. I think this conference really started on the other side of that statement. I think that this conference started to go back to the idea in the Lerner and Loewe musical: "I don't want to hear any more words, there isn't one I haven't heard—show me." And therefore we have talked about various specific things that happen and can be caused to happen in the schools and in colleges concerned with the mundane business of schools and colleges, curriculum, teachers, students, organization, who goes to school with whom, and these kinds of things. Now these don't make as high-sounding words as that statement has in it, I'm quite willing to agree. And yet it seems to me if we're going to get about the business of implementing that statement, we really have to talk about the kinds of things we've talked about—inadequately to some extent, and with much disorganization, for which I'll take the responsibility. But that's the kind of difficult, stretching conversation that has to take place if the generalizations that you find in a statement like that *are* going to make any dent in American attitudes.

It seems to me that our possibility of making a dent relies primarily on the individuals who are here and their willingness to subscribe to an ultimate document which will come out of this, on the spread of that document and on its filtering down into the system as all these documents do, and on getting it made use of here and there—by one school board or one association or one Commissioner of Education or whoever it may be. I think we might have made a small dent on things by the lines of the UNESCO statement, but my guess is that had we produced a document like that for the United States, we wouldn't have done education as much service as we have by this more detailed conversation.

Bruno Bitker: Let me finish this. I did not intend that we should write another statement on race. You don't have to write it—it has been written a hundred times. I'm talking about how do you get the idea to the American public.

Franklin Roosevelt: I think that Mr. Bitker has hit on one thing. I think that this conference could easily recommend to the President's Commission, of which two members are here present, that they urge the Commission to pass out our conference report to the institutions of higher learning, to high schools, and even perhaps to primary schools throughout the country with a request and a suggestion that each of these institutions have a day or two-day session of self-examination, using our report as a starting point for their particular problem. Secondly, I would suggest that it be recommended to the Commission that they seek through conferences and other means to get the news media, television, radio, and newspapers, to realize their full responsibility in this area.

Christopher Edley: It seems to me that Mr. Bitker has tried to bring us back to the topic Ken Clark tried at least three times yesterday to get us to discuss. And several other people in a different context tried to get us to agree on priorities.

What you want us to do is a very difficult undertaking. And at the risk of being shot down by twenty guns, I will share with you the idea that I have developed after years of frustration.

I'm convinced that the way you eliminate prejudice and racism in America is not by talking and education and explanation. I think that you have to start with a simple cliché like God, motherhood, or country. You have to have something that has a noble ring. And it seems to me that what this country needs is a movement, and I don't know that this is the appropriate group to try to sponsor it. This country needs a movement. The way to eliminate prejudice is to smother it. If we could bring about a climate in this country where no one could express a prejudicial point without being challenged, we would begin to drive prejudice underground. And I submit to you that prejudice unexpressed and unacted upon dies—it doesn't fester and grow—it dies. Now this is high-sounding, and I don't expect people to agree with such a simplistic solution. But I really believe that you can stamp it out. And if you look at our national figures today, there are certain people who cannot make a prejudicial remark. Many of our Governors, the President, many responsible Senators are precluded in their public lives from ever making a prejudiced public statement, and if they make a statement that sounds like it's prejudicial, they're called on it and the next day, as General de Gaulle found, it was necessary to recant. So we don't allow them to get away with anything. But at the lower levels, over the dinner table . . .

Franklin Roosevelt: The citizen level . . .

Christopher Edley: At the citizen level, we say it's perfectly all right for a bigot to express his bigoted thoughts. If you're anti-Negro you can speak out against the Negro at supper. The simplicity of the idea I submit to you is the thing that gives it some national potential for changing the climate.

II

The Agenda
for Action

The Agenda for Action

I. Definition of Racism, Background: Rationale

The Kerner Report of the Commission on Civil Disorders and other studies confirm the reality that American education is infected with the pervasive social disease of racism. Racism is one of the most virulent forms of class distinctions in American life; it is widespread, and its manifestations are both apparent and seemingly intractable in the United States. Since education traditionally, often passively, reflects the values and beliefs of society, the entrenchment of racism in education is an indication of its pervasiveness in the society at large; it is also a challenge to education not merely to reflect society but to take the leadership in changing those values.

American educational institutions reflect racial and class distinctions even though those responsible for them often claim that they are seeking to erase the problem. The public schools remain in large part segregated by race, and many of the minority-group schools have the worst facilities, the highest teacher turnover, and the least support. These facts, in turn, raise questions about the school support policies at local, state, and federal levels of government.

The existence of these distinctions governs the fact that the quality of education provided for American children differs according to their racial, economic, and social class status. Children of lower status generally perform academically at a level lower on the average than children of middle and upper status.

The present organization, financing, and governance of local public school systems have failed to remedy these per-

149

sistent educational inequities. New state equalization and new federal aid equalization are needed in the face of the inability or unwillingness of local communities to expand their level of support for education. A major domestic development plan for educational policies and programs, including large-scale demonstrations and funds for experimentation in leader and teacher training, is required to redress these conditions of educational inequity harmful to children and detrimental to a free society. The consequences of inequity are clear. They include flagrant damage to minority-group children. They also include insidious and subtle damage to the children of the white majority.

The patterns of injustice associated with racial and class distinctions present a grave threat to all Americans, and to the stability and viability of the American democratic system. Racism in American education not only reflects the racism in the society but also reinforces and perpetuates it, breeding ignorance, superstitions, provincialism, and irrational fears and hatreds.

The highest priority must be given to determining and implementing realistic methods for eliminating both flagrant and subtle forms of racism from education and for controlling its virulent manifestations in the society. Education must recognize and accept as a primary responsibility the need to liberate the human mind and spirit, and must assume the initiative in developing the positive potential of human beings, freeing them from the constrictions of ignorance, and its non-adaptive consequences—irrational fear and hatred.

AREAS FOR ACTION

Relevant actions for the elimination of racism in American education must be planned and implemented to achieve these ends:

   1. to effect attitudinal changes;

2. to bring about structural and institutional changes;
3. to bring about changes designed to improve the quality of education.

Action must be taken at all levels of leadership—federal, state, and local—and on all levels of education—public and private; elementary and secondary; colleges, universities, and professional schools; general adult education through the public media.

II. SPECIFIC ACTION RECOMMENDATIONS

1. Attitudinal Change. The objective of attitudinal change will include:

   a. curriculum revision on all levels, to ensure that the substance of education, particularly in history, the social sciences, and the humanities, is made more relevant to the questions and imperatives of social justice and social change;

   b. achievement of high standards of scholarship and research on the role and influence of social class and race in the American experience;

   c. revision and expansion of teacher training curricula to include significant content in cultural anthropology, ethnology, social psychology, history, and the relevant behavioral sciences and with particular emphasis on the type of actual experiences with and field training in school and communities;

   d. development of a massive program of adult and public education on the problems and the negative social consequences of racism, a program that will be pragmatic in character, designed to make American ideals real for all people by clarifying direct relationships between positive self-interest and racial equity, between maturity of attitude and commitment to racial justice, immaturity of attitude and racial prejudice;

e. development of an extensive program of education against racism within and through the schools and colleges and other institutions utilizing the advanced techniques of mass communication;

f. commitment to the objectives of public school integration—immediately among schools in cities where this is now possible; and as quickly as possible where, even with most vigorous efforts, more time will be required. Coexisting with such plans must be the parallel purpose of securing quality education for all pupils, especially for those in schools which, during the interim, remain segregated. States should require their school districts to move forward on both of these fundamental objectives and should provide financial incentives for doing so. The federal government should likewise provide incentives for state and local governments to develop concrete programs which meet the twin objectives of integration and quality.

2. Structural and Fiscal Changes

a. State authorities should move to assume tax responsibility for local education and use their power and their funds to restructure public education so that it serves the children from low-income and minority groups as well as it serves children of the middle class, and so that discrimination, segregation, and racist attitudes are reduced.

b. Additional federal funds should flow through the states to advance those ends. The federal government should play a growing role in equalizing educational opportunity by providing funds through equalization formulas based on the states' capacity to support quality education, and by requiring the use of federal funds within states to buttress educational opportunity for the children of the poor and for those children against whom society now discriminates.

c. Federal and state resources must be used to encourage new educational systems in areas of chronic poor student achievement as alternatives to the present system of public schools. Such alternative public education systems would provide maximum options for equal educational opportunities. These systems should be demonstration projects to determine whether they do, in fact, lead to increased efficiency and quality of education for children of various economic levels. These new efforts can have many manifestations. They can be operated by any agency, public or private, existing or newly established. They can experiment with novel systems of teaching and learning. (Tuition grants can be provided for use in certified institutions.) Economic motivation can be used as a stimulus for both teacher and student in a reward system directly related to pupil performance.

d. School construction, whether financed by federal, state, or local funds, can offer a way to dual objectives of improving the quality of education and seeking the reduction of racial isolation. New programs to rebuild the schools should:

1. bring together the city with the suburb in joint planning and in use of facilities;
2. ensure that racial segregation is not frozen by faulty placement of facilities;
3. provide special facilities for science, vocational education, and for a variety of curricula areas far superior to those found in the usual city or suburban school;
4. give premium levels of support to projects whose site

and plans reduce racial isolation and provide education more pertinent to the needs of educationally deprived children;

5. support regional planning for higher education;
6. provide compensatory programs which can finance modernization of buildings and facilities.

e. Successful models of central city schools need to be developed through a dozen or more different, cooperative federal and state plans. Such models could encompass groups of 20,000 or more children from preschool age, three years old, to college-age youth. Each separate model should be financed for at least a ten-year period. No limitation on policy or funds should be required with the exception of a prohibition against the reinforcement of racism. The form of governance could also be varied, including the traditional school board structure or new, independent, nonprofit corporation control or structures designed by private business with encouraging tax incentives.

3. Improving Quality of Education

Educational policies and programs designed to improve the academic performance of minority-group children and to deepen the social sensitivity of white children must be planned and implemented. Such plans should parallel efforts to achieve the goals of a nonracist public educational system pursued with increasing vigor and without equivocation. In that regard we recommend:

a. the development of more realistic and relevant programs of preparation for teachers, incorporating courses in anthropology, ethnology, social psychology, history, and other appropriate social sciences for prospective teachers; and exposure of teachers-in-training to field experience in urban communities and to the realities of central city and rural schools;

b. the establishment in all urban public school systems of a massive program of inservice training for teachers to compensate for their deficits in the behavioral sciences and in the understanding of human differences and potentialities, and gaining an intimate knowledge of their pupils and the communities from which they come;

c. a program of tutoring in urban schools under high school and college students who would serve as models of idealism and commitment;

d. a program of community participation in the schools, including:

1. decentralization of large urban school districts;
2. volunteers and teachers' aides from the community serving with professional teachers in classrooms;
3. courses for parents; and
4. channeling neighborhood residents to health, employment, and welfare services within the schools, and unifying schools as a community educational and service resource;

e. the implementation of a realistic system of accountability tied to some basis for the evaluation of the performance and competence of teachers and superiors. As it now stands, groups, organizations, and unions have fought successfully against differential pay or "merit pay" increases on the grounds that such systems would lead to administrative abuses and preferences. It is difficult to assess the competence of an individual teacher in individual cases by the academic performance of his students. The present demands for decentralization and more direct community controls of the schools, particularly in low-income and minority-group areas of the larger cities of America, are essentially concerned with developing some system and criteria by which performance of teachers will be evaluated. These demands cannot be ignored and will increase. It follows, therefore, that it is now incumbent on education to find rational and realistic solutions to this problem.

Teachers might well be required to progress professionally through ranks of differentiation of assignment and status that would be dependent on quality of performance and rewarded by advance in income. Teacher compensation needs to be raised, generally, to make it possible for teaching to become competitive as a profession with other opportunities favorable to college graduates, as it now is not. Teaching now, therefore, tends to attract those of lower status, who view it as a status and security advance, and who often tend to reject the lower-status students they encounter in their classes. Such persons may bring narrow, prejudicial attitudes to their classrooms. A way must be found to bring to the profession more highly motivated college students of idealism and competence to build the teaching profession, instead of the present token number of such persons. Highly motivated teachers should be the norm;

f. revision and development of textbooks and other educational material to reflect the reality of American ethnic diversity so as to build a sense of positive identity in all children, to strengthen social sensitivity and empathy for the struggle for justice and democracy, and to present to children a realistic portrait of America's history—its successes and failures, its controversies and unsolved problems.

The rewriting of history books or new presentations of reading materials can, however, err just as seriously by romanticizing the history of minority groups. The solution is to tell it "like it was," to tell it "like it is," and to tell why it wasn't told before. The real story of the degradation of black people by white, the history of prejudice, and the account of the nature of prejudice, is a powerful instrument for building social understanding.

4. Actions Specific to Higher Education

The persistence of racism in American life reflects, among other causes, the default of American higher education or its inability to exercise aggressive leadership. Because higher education facilities remain largely partially segregated, and the anachronisms "Negro colleges" and "white colleges" continue, we, therefore recommend:

  a. that American higher education move toward the elimination of every vestige of racism;
  b. that programs be instituted as rapidly as possible so that "Negro colleges" and "white colleges" free themselves of anachronistic racial designation and characteristic, and that colleges generally demonstrate both quality of education and a repudiation of racism in their organizational structure through demonstrable increase in the number of minority-group members in their faculties and administration, their boards of trustees, and their undergraduate, graduate, and professional student bodies. Colleges should assume leadership in demanding that elementary and secondary schools eliminate racism; they should intensify special interim college preparatory educational programs to compensate for the present educational deficits of minority-group children and to enable them to compete under a single standard with more privileged children; they should admit educationally disadvantaged students upon the basis of potential and provide them with special programs to compensate for the educational deprivation of their earlier years;

c. that college and university teaching and research in the
social and behavioral sciences, history, the humanities
and the arts, and research be made more vital in terms
of contemporary social issues and problems, in terms of
the need for effective social action and democratic social
change. The concern of the present generation of American college students that their education be made more
relevant to society and to racial and social justice should
be mobilized in behalf of such a strengthened program.
Students should be given credit for curriculum-related
work in communities. Faculties should be encouraged
and rewarded for research, action, and service in urban
areas. Colleges and universities should contribute their
resources to appropriate community programs and activities.

III. Related Problems

The possibility of conflict between certain specific interim objectives and the over-all goal of liberating American education
from racism needs to be faced. These dangers must be noted:

1. Racial segregation in schools may be temporarily or per-
manently increased through adoption of tactical and interim
efforts to increase quality of education for minority-group
children.
2. Compensatory and enrichment programs could obscure the
basic issue of the incompatibility between high-quality education for all children and the existence of segregated
schools.
3. Decentralization of schools could reinforce the neighbor-
hood-school concept, which is related to the perpetuation
of a segregated school system.
4. Remedial and special-admission programs could perpetuate
double racial standards for judging academic performance

of minority students, thereby reinforcing racial stereotyping and racism in education.

As long as racially segregated schools exist in the context of a racially segregated society, it will be difficult to free American education from racism. The above analysis and recommendations are presented under the assumption that education and educational institutions can provide our society with the guidance and educational programs essential to the maintenance of dynamic democracy imperative for humanity and national stability.

Index

70 71 72 73   12 11 10 9 8 7 6 5 4 3 2 1

DATE DUE